LONGMAN IMPRINT

Intensive Care

Four TV plays
edited by
Michael Church

Longman

Contents

	page
Introduction	1

Intensive Care — 3
Alan Bennett

An Introduction by Alan Bennett	4
The play	8

The Flip Side of Dominick Hide — 47
Jeremy Paul and Alan Gibson

An Introduction by Alan Gibson	48
An Introduction by Jeremy Paul	51
The play	54

Looking for Vicky — 111
Jane Hollowood

An Introduction by Jane Hollowood	112
The play	116

A Night of the Campaign — 149
Robin Glendinning and Leonard Kingston

An Introduction by Robin Glendinning	150
The play	154

Coursework assignments for GCSE	196
Wider reading	201

Introduction

Sitting at home watching television, you're part of the audience for the biggest theatre in the world. And, like everyone else sitting in their home, you're in a front-row seat. The actors don't have to shout to make you hear, or give long speeches so that you'll get the point: all they have to do is whisper a word or two, or raise an eyebrow, to let you know they're excited, or angry, or sad.

Television plays are written in a quite different way from stage plays. This means that you must read them differently – you must be ready to catch every hint of a new mood, or a new twist in the story. A single line can change everything that has happened so far. Dramatic writing for television is never 'wordy'.

And plays on film can do things which stage plays can never do. On stage, unless the director decides to do clever things with props and lighting, the action must stay rooted in one spot – a shop, a bedroom, a bar. And once the actors are on stage they have to stay there for a while, otherwise the whole thing can become ridiculous, with people running on and off like clockwork toys.

Like the cinema, television sets the action free, so that the writers can take us wherever they want. The authors of *Dominick Hide*, for instance, can carry us in a flash from earth to outer space and back again, or from the 1980s to far in the future. In a few moments Alan Bennett can take us not only from Midgley's home to hospital and back, but off into Midgley's childhood in the form of a dream. In *Looking for Vicky* the tension is screwed to fever pitch as the film cuts from the menacing figure in the phone box to the ringing phone and back again. The fourth play in this book moves through the dark streets of Belfast, stopping at house after house to show how neighbours disagree over politics.

Political disagreements, and differing attitudes to life, are what all these plays are about. Dominick rebels against his family in order to go back and explore the differences between his world and that of his great-grandparents. Philippa and her mother clash violently over Red – until they each learn a little wisdom. Midgley is at war with everybody – his wife, his son, his uncle, his father – until he takes a big step and breaks free. In *A Night of the Campaign* Susan and her parents quarrel over politics and homework as teenagers and parents do everywhere.

In these pages you will find that many worlds meet, clash, and sometimes, in unexpected ways, become reconciled.

Michael Church

Intensive Care
(or Father, Father Burning Bright)

by Alan Bennett

An Introduction by Alan Bennett

A playwright is not the best person to talk about his own work for the simple reason that he is often unaware of what he has written. Someone (I think, Tom Stoppard) has compared the playwright confronted by his critics to a passage through Customs. Under the impression he has nothing to declare the playwright heads confidently for the Green exit. Alerted (and irritated) by this air of confidence an official of the Customs and Excise steps forward and asks our writer formally, 'Have you any contraband?' 'No', smiles the playwright! 'Very well,' says the officer, 'kindly open your suitcase.' Happy to comply (he has nothing to be ashamed of after all) the playwright throws back the lid. Whereupon to his horror there lie revealed a pair of disgustingly dirty underpants and some extremely pungent socks. The playwright is covered in confusion; for though these underpants are undoubtedly his and the socks too, nevertheless he has no recollection of having packed them, still less of giving them pride of place on top of his belongings. The customs officer sniffs (as well he might). However since there is (as yet) no law against the import of dirty underpants or smelly socks the officer gingerly puts them on one side and delves further into the playwright's case.

The next revelation is some photographs. These too take the playwright by surprise. Had he packed them? Surely not. But they are most certainly his; this is a photograph of his father and here are three photographs of his mother and at least half a dozen of himself. 'Rather fond of ourselves, aren't we sir?' murmurs the customs man insolently. The playwright stammers some excuse, only thankful that the snaps are after all quite decent. But his relief is premature because, after sifting through yet more soiled clothing the customs man now unearths another photograph: it is the playwright again, only this time he has his trousers down, he is smiling and with every appearance of pride he is showing his bottom to the camera. Now not only does the playwright not remember packing this photograph, he doesn't even remember it being taken. But that is him; those are his trousers; that is his smile and yes, that without question, is his bottom. 'One of our holiday snaps, is it, sir?' sneers the customs officer. 'I should keep that covered up if I were you. We all have one, you know.'

And so the embarrassing examination goes on, the searcher uncovering ever more outrageous items . . . ideas the playwright thought he had long since discarded, an old marriage, a dead teacher and even a body or two, locked in a long forgotten embrace, none of which the playwright ever dreamed of packing but which somehow have found their way into this commodious suitcase, his play.

So you see there is not all that much point in my telling you what *Intensive Care* is about or what I have put in my particular suitcase. I can list some of the contents of course (all fairly obvious) and tell you a little about how they relate to my own circumstances and experience, but you, like the customs officer, may come across something more incriminating, and remember, your list of contents will be just as valid as mine. No. All a playwright can hope for is that, whatever he has wittingly or unwittingly included, his play will relate to, will chime in with the experience and circumstances of his audience.

To begin with the father in the play: he is not in the least like my own father. Once I was through my teens I got on well with my Dad and he never filled me with that sense of hopeless inadequacy for which Denis Midgley blames his father. Still, re-reading the play some five years after I wrote it I can see that my father has managed to get into the play, only he is wearing Uncle Ernest's hat. That is often the way in plays and novels. Characters are seldom yanked out of life and hi-jacked unchanged into art, shoved just as they are onto the stage or in front of the camera. The playwright has to take tham to Costume first and Make-up in order to alter their appearance; sometimes he even takes them to a surgeon to change their sex. So that when the writer's finished with them they come on as someone far removed from the character they began as. So my father turns into Uncle Ernest. 'I can't understand how your Aunty Kitty's managed to escape strangulation for so long' is just the way my father talked; like Uncle Ernest he called his younger brother 'butt', a north country version of 'mate', and like him he was embarrassed by emotion and sat by his own brother's bedside as much at a loss as Uncle Ernest, turning his trilby hat in his big red hands, knowing there was nothing to be said or done, and that if there was he would be too shy to say it.

There are other sons and other fathers in the play besides Denis and the dying Mr Midgley. Denis himself has a son, Colin, with whom he gets on no better than his father got on with him (and in much the same way). Uncle Ernest has a son, Hartley, and their relations are none too good either. Hartley has a son, Mark, who plainly regards his father as a bit of a pill. And so on. But of course Denis gets on fine with Uncle Ernest, who is not his father, and were Mr Midgley up and about he and Hartley wouldn't waste time on feelings of guilt and inadequacy. As uncle and nephew they would act like normal people. But parents aren't normal people and nor are children. In one of my other plays a girl remarks 'My problem is, I hate my loved ones' and while things are not quite as bad as that in *Intensive Care*, relations between children and their parents are characterised by shame, embarrassment and boredom on the children's side and resentment and envy on the parents', with (I hope) somewhere in the undergrowth love and affection managing to survive.

My favourite character in the play is Aunty Kitty. She's a terrible woman, prejudiced, sentimental and convinced that whatever the situation, even a deathbed, she is the central figure. A real pain in life, in art such characters are sheer joy. In the television film she was played by Thora Hird as a woman who was always eating a sweet or blowing on a steaming cup of coffee, even her noblest moments nudged into the ridiculous by an inappropriate licorice allsort.

Whether I am like Denis Midgley it is not for me to say though it was sheer accident that I ended up playing the part. Finding himself unable to cast Denis, the director, Gavin Millar tried to persuade me to play it. My first impulse was to say no, knowing I would be embarrassed by the bedroom scene with Valery (Julie Walters). Then I decided this was cowardly and not a reason at all and agreed to do it. However I had waited too long; Gavin had begun to go off the idea just as I had started to get keen on it. The upshot was I ended up auditioning in order to prove that I could play a part in my own play. Even so I got more and more nervous as we drew near to the bedroom scene, which was scheduled for the last day of filming. Before we did the main bedroom scenes I had to stand (in my shirttails) in the bathroom and deliver lines off camera while Julie was filmed undressing and getting into bed. It was bitterly cold and the shots took a long time so that when the point came for me to be filmed joining her all embarrassment had long since fled and I was just happy to be getting into somewhere warm.

Alan Bennett, 1987

INTENSIVE CARE

The Cast

Father (Frank Midgley – age 72)
Denis Midgley (age 39. School teacher)
Mrs Joyce Midgley
Valery Lightfoot (night nurse)
Aunty Kitty (age 70's)
Uncle Ernest (age 74)
Hartley (Uncle Ernest's son)
Jean (Hartley's wife)
Mark (Hartley's son)
Elizabeth (Hartley's daughter)
Alice Duckworth (age late 50's/early 60's)
Colin Midgley (Denis's teenage son)
Mrs Midgley's mother

Voice over
Teacher
Miss Tunstall (school secretary)
Mrs Azakwale (black parent)
Mr Horsfall (police sgt. parent)
Headmaster
Denis's mother (old)
Denis's mother (young)
Nurse 1
Nurse 2
Indian doctor
Fat man
Young man
Nurse 3
Porter 2
Nurse 4
Woman on sticks
Nurse 5
Nurse 6 (Maureen)
Orderly
Woman on telephone
Very young doctor
Night matron
Denis Midgley as a boy
Hospital administrator
Young man or Colin's girl friend

Intensive Care

1 A Hospital Corridor

A long featureless corridor in a modern hospital, empty, with double doors at the end. Suddenly the doors swing open and a trolley with an elderly man on it is pushed madly along by a resuscitation team.

2 Midgley's Kitchen

Midgley, a man of thirty-nine sits at a kitchen table, looking into the camera. He has his hat and coat on. A carving knife is in front of him on the table.

MIDGLEY I just never expected it.
VOICE OVER On the many occasions Midgley had killed his father, death always came easily. He died neatly, promptly and without a struggle. But it was not like his father to die like that. Nor did he.
MIDGLEY The timing is good. It's only my father who would stage his farewell in the middle of Meet The Parents week.

Mrs Midgley seizes the carving knife and slices the crust viciously for Midgley's sandwiches. She looks disgusted.

3 Midgley's School

Parents are coming in to the hall, watched by Midgley and another teacher.

MIDGLEY Observe how young the parents are getting. Fathers in particular. They even have permed hair, the odd ear-ring ... features I still find it hard to forgive in the children.

Miss Tunstall, the school secretary, hands them several folders.

TEACHER I saw one with a swastika necklace.
MIDGLEY A boy?
TEACHER A parent.

MIDGLEY There's a mother wandering round with green hair.
MISS T Not just green. *Bright* green. And then you wonder the girls get pregnant.

In the hall tables are set up with rows of chairs, some filled with parents wanting to see teachers, including Mrs Azakwale.

MRS A Coretta's bin havin' these massive monthlies, Mr Midgley. Believe me en twenty years I en never seen menstruatin' like it.
MIDGLEY It's her poor showing in Use of English that worries me.
MRS A She bin wadin' about in blood to her ankles, Mr Midgley. I 'en never out of the launderette.

Behind Mrs Azakwale, waiting his turn, is a large, dour man, Mr Horsfall, a police sergeant. He catches Midgley's eye and shakes his head in despair.

MIDGLEY I worry about Coretta's attention span. (*Coretta is paying no attention at this moment either*) It's very short.
MRS A I'm saying: She bin concentratin' on gettin' through puberty. Once that's out of the way I reckon it's all plain sailin'. Now then, Coretta, pigeon, where's this Computer Sciences gentlemen?

Next in the queue is Mr Horsfall and his son.

HORSFALL He had every chance. Every chance in the world. Chance after chance after chance. I've lost count of the number of chances he's had.
MIDGLEY Martin is a little young for his age.
HORSFALL Martin? Is that what you call him?
MIDGLEY That's his name.
HORSFALL His name is Horsfall. Martin is what we call him, his mother and me. For your purposes I should have thought Horsfall was sufficient. Are you married? And you teach him English? He can scarcely string two words together. (*to his son*) Why Martin? Why? I can. Your father. I have to. People making their statements, who is it who finds them the right word? Me. I can put words together. At four o'clock in the morning after a day spent combing copses and dragging ponds, making house to house enquiries I can do it. The father. But not the son. Why? Well? Say something Martin. (*Martin says nothing*) I mean: a school like this. Soccer facilities: tip top. Swimming bath:

tip top. Gymnasium: tip top. You want to be grateful. We never had chances like that did we, Midgley?

It's Midgley's turn to say nothing. Miss Tunstall comes up, waits a moment then makes little waving signs behind Mr Horsfall's head, who, a policeman and ever alert to mockery, turns round.

MISS T (*addressing Horsfall, not Midgley*) The hospital's just rung. Mr Midgley's father's been taken ill. (*only then does she look at Midgley*) Your father's been taken ill.

4 School Office

Midgley is on the telephone. Miss Tunstall is sitting at the desk, waiting to start typing.

MIDGLEY They're ringing the ward. It's a stroke, apparently. And he's had a fall.

MISS T You want to pray it's not his hip. That's generally the weak spot. The pelvis heals in no time, surprisingly. Mother broke her pelvis. I thought it was the beginning of the end.

MIDGLEY (*on the telephone*) Hello?

MISS T She took a nasty tumble in Safeways last week. They do when they get older. It's what you have to expect. I'm reconciled to it now. Their bones get brittle.

She cracks her fingers and begins to type.

MIDGLEY (*on the telephone*) No, I don't want Maintenance. I want Ward 7.

Miss Tunstall stops typing.

MISS T It's these ancillary workers. Holding the country to ransom. Other people's suffering is their bread and butter.

She starts typing again softly.

MIDGLEY (*on the telephone*) Midgley. Midgley. (*She stops typing*) I'm his son. (*listens*) I see. Thank you. He's critical. They say it's touch and go.

MISS T How old is he?

MIDGLEY Seventy-two.

MISS T My mother's eighty-two. Life is unfair.

Midgley is still standing by the telephone when the headmaster breezes in.

HEADMASTER   On the 'phone again, Midgley. I'm the one who has to go cap in hand to the Finance Committee.
MISS T   Mr Midgley's father's ill. It's touch and go.

She starts typing like the wind. Headmaster takes Midgley into his study.

5 Headmaster's Study

HEADMASTER   Of course you can go. Of course you must go. One's father. There can be no question. It's awkward of course. But then it always is. Was he getting on in years?
MIDGLEY   Seventy-four.
HEADMASTER   Seventy-four. Once upon a time I thought that was old.

He looks at the timetable, a vast, complicated affair.

HEADMASTER   Let me see. It's English, Integrated Humanities and Creative Arts. Nothing else is there?
MIDGLEY   Environmental Studies.
HEADMASTER   (*groaning*) That's the bluebottle in the vaseline. Pilbeam's off on a course. That's the trouble with the environment. It involves going on courses. I shall be glad when it's a proper subject and confined to the text-books. Ah well. I have no parents. They were despatched years ago. A flying bomb.
MIDGLEY   He must have been lying there two days.
HEADMASTER   A familiar scenario. Isolated within the community. Alone in the crowd. You must not feel guilty.
MIDGLEY   I generally go over at weekends.
HEADMASTER   It will give Tomlinson an opportunity to do some of his weird and wonderful permutations with the timetable. Though I fear this one will tax even Tomlinson's talents.

They go back into the office.

6 School Office

HEADMASTER   One must hope it is not as grave as it appears. One must hope he turns the corner. Corners seem to have gone out nowadays. In the old days the sick were always turning

	them. Illness now much more of a straight road. Why is that?
MIDGLEY	Antibiotics?
HEADMASTER	Ye-es. One has the impression modern medicine encourages patients to loiter. Mistakenly one feels. God speed: (*he looks at the notice Miss Tunstall has been typing*) Ah yes. Hooliganism in the swimming baths. The changing rooms. I'm not sure if we've couched this in strong enough terms, Daphne.
MISS T	It's as you dictated it.
HEADMASTER	I have no doubt. But I feel more stongly about it now. Nothing else is there, Midgley?

Midgley shakes his head, smiles weakly at Miss Tunstall and goes out.

HEADMASTER	A boy slips. Is pushed. We are talking about concussion. A broken neck. A fatality, Daphne. I intend to nail the culprits. I want them to know they will be crucified.
MISS T	Shall I put that?

The headmaster looks sharply at her.

HEADMASTER	First this business of Midgley père. Ask Tomlinson to step over, will you. Tell him to bring his coloured pencils. And a rubber.

7 Midgley's Kitchen

As in Scene 2. Midgley is sitting in his coat at the kitchen table, the carving knife in front of him while his wife prepares his sandwiches.

MIDGLEY	I have treated him so badly. All along.

Mrs Midgley says nothing, but grimly spreads the bread.

MIDGLEY	I wanted to go over this last weekend. It's my fault.
MRS MIDGLEY	Tomato or my jam?
MIDGLEY	Tomato. I just never expected it.
MRS MIDGLEY	I did. Last time I went over he came to the door to wave me off. He's never done that before. I think people know.

Pause.

MIDGLEY He does come to the door. He invariably comes to the door.

Mrs Midgley shakes her head sensitively.

MRS MIDGLEY He was trying to tell me something. I know a farewell when I see one.

She puts the sandwiches, flask, in front of him and waits.

MRS MIDGLEY Is there anything else you want?

8 Midgley's Home

A little later: Midgley still hasn't left. Mrs Midgley is dusting now, and her mother is asleep in a chair.

MIDGLEY I'm not going to let him down. I want to be there when he goes. He loved me.

Mrs Midgley picks up an item and dusts beneath it, viciously.

MIDGLEY Don't you think so?
MRS MIDGLEY I do. Though why, I can't imagine. It's not as if you take after him.

She dusts something else.

MRS MIDGLEY One little bit.

Mrs Midgley's mother wakes up.

MOTHER Is it Saturday today?

9 Midgley's Home

Midgley goes and sits on the stairs. Mrs Midgley is out of shot, still cleaning.

MRS MIDGLEY He had strength. Our Colin is going to be strong. He loved Colin.
MIDGLEY Does he know?
MRS MIDGLEY Yes. It hasn't hit him yet. When it does he's going to be heartbroken. They both are. Poor old Frank.
MIDGLEY I've never understood why you call him Frank. He's my Father.
MRS MIDGLEY He has a name. Frank is his name.

MIDGLEY You're the only one who uses it. Everybody else calls him Dad. Else Grandad.
MRS MIDGLEY He's not Dad is he? I call him Frank because that's the name of a person. To me he is a person. That's why we get on.

Mrs Midgley's mother appears at the door of the sitting room.

MOTHER Joyce.
MRS MIDGLEY Coming, mother.

10 Colin's Bedroom

Midgley walks into his teenage son, Colin's bedroom: Colin switches off the music he has just had on very loud.

COLIN Dad, I've told you before. Don't just walk in. Knock.
MIDGLEY I did knock.
COLIN This is my room. I could be doing anything.
MIDGLEY I've got to go over to Bradford. To the hospital. Grandad's poorly.
COLIN I know. Mum said. I thought you'd have gone by now. I'm really sorry.

Midgley goes out and the music starts again instantly.

11 Midgley's Kitchen

Midgley goes back into the kitchen.

MIDGLEY Why don't you come?
MRS MIDGLEY With Mother? How can I?
MIDGLEY Ta ra, then.

He kisses her and goes to the back door and opens it, then stops.

MIDGLEY Anyway it isn't.
MRS MIDGLEY It isn't what?
MIDGLEY It isn't why you get on. Treating him like a person. You get on because you both despise me. That's why he gets on with our Colin. He despises me too.
MRS MIDGLEY Your father is seventy-two. He is dying, possibly. A good, good man is dying. And you hang about here resenting the fact that he and I were friends and that he was friends with your son, who is lying upstairs at this moment,

genuinely heartbroken. I seem to have married someone very low down in the evolutionary chain. You might want one or two tissues.

She stuffs some tissues into his pocket.

MIDGLEY When you and he were together I didn't exist.

MRS MIDGLEY I am married to the cupboard under the sink. He is *dying*. Will you exist now? Will that satisfy you?

MIDGLEY I'll make it right. I'll be there when he goes. I'll hold his hand. I shan't let him down. If I let him down now I'll never be able to make it right. He'd stay with me the rest of my life. I did love him, Joyce.

MRS MIDGLEY I would like him to stay with you for the rest of your life. I hope he does stay with you for the rest of your life. As an example. As somebody to live up to. I think of his kindness. His unselfishness. His unflagging courtesy. The only incredible thing is that someone so truly saintly should have produced such a pill of a son. But I suppose that's your mother.

MIDGLEY Shut up about my mother. My mother is dead.

MRS MIDGLEY So is he, virtually. Dawdling. Go.

MIDGLEY Then things will change, you'll see. I'll change. I'll be a different person. I can . . . go. Live. Start!

He kisses her quickly and goes out.

MRS MIDGLEY (*shouting after him*) Start? You're thirty-nine!

12 Road to Bradford

On the road from Hull to Bradford, Midgley sees an old man waiting to cross at a zebra. As the man goes across he holds up his hand to stop oncoming traffic and suddenly changes into Midgley's father. Then Midgley sees his father at every turn: sitting on a seat, waiting at a bus stop, and then carrying the shopping bag while out with Midgley's mother. Midgley begins to cry.

13 Hospital Waiting Room

Midgley is sitting with Aunty Kitty, in her seventies, his father's sister.

AUNTY KITTY I thought you'd have been here a bit since. I was here at

INTENSIVE CARE

	3 o'clock. You'll notice a big change. He's not like my brother. He's not the Frank I knew. I don't dislike this colour scheme. I always liked oatmeal. The doctor's black.
MIDGLEY	Did he know you?
AUNTY KITTY	The nurse says he doesn't know anybody but I think he knew me. The Duchess of Kent opened the unit apparently. The kidney department's world-famous. (*A nurse comes in.*) This is my nephew, Mr Midgley's son. Your father's got a room to himself, love.
NURSE 1	They all do, at this stage.

14 Hospital Room

Midgley goes into the room where his father is lying. His father is lying motionless with his eyes open, and with a monitor on his chest.

MIDGLEY Dad. Dad. It's me, Denis. I've come. I've come, Dad. It's all right.

He pulls his chair up to the bed and holds his father's hand.

MIDGLEY	I'm sorry Dad.
NURSE 2	(*looking in*) Are you next of kin?
MIDGLEY	Son.
NURSE 2	Not too long.

Midgley waits, holding his father's hand.

Aunty Kitty comes in.

AUNTY KITTY	I wonder where he is? What does that look on his face mean?
MIDGLEY	It means that he is dying and it's my fault.

A nurse comes and stands at the door and they go out to the waiting room again.

AUNTY KITTY It's just a case of waiting now. There's a lot of waiting done in hospitals. Ninety per cent of it's waiting.

Stroking the upholstery.

I suppose you'd call this russet. Would you call this chestnut or russet? (*pause*) I always thought I'd be the one to go first. They've never got to the bottom of my

	complaint. They lowered a microscope down my throat, but that drew a blank as well. Mr Penry-Jones said they were baffled. I asked the nurse. I said, 'Is he just unconscious or is he in a coma?' She didn't know. They don't get the training now.
MIDGLEY	Aunty.
AUNTY KITTY	She wasn't black. Black she'd have had some excuse.
MIDGLEY	Aunty. What was my Dad like?
AUNTY KITTY	He never had a wrong word for anybody, your Dad. He'd do anybody a good turn. Shovel their snow. Fetch their coal in. He was a saint. (*pause*) You take after your mother more.
MIDGLEY	I feel I lack his sterling qualities. Grit. Patience. That willingness to shoulder other people's burdens. Virtues bred out of adversity.
AUNTY KITTY	I think you change when you go to university.
MIDGLEY	Deprivation, for instance. I was never deprived, Aunty Kitty. That way he deprived me, do you see?
AUNTY KITTY	I should have gone to secondary school. I left school at thirteen same as your Dad. Muriel Brunskill, she stopped on. They went into fancy goods. They have a shop in the Headrow.
MIDGLEY	I know I had it easier than my Dad. But I was grateful. I didn't take it for granted. It's not particularly enjoyable, education.
AUNTY KITTY	You used to look bonny in your blazer.
MIDGLEY	He gave me what he'd wanted. Why should that be enjoyable?
AUNTY KITTY	You ought to be ringing round. Telling Ernest, Hartley and Christine. Robin's just got his bronze medal.
MIDGLEY	I'll wait and see the doctor first.
AUNTY KITTY	You'd have thought they'd have had all these complaints licked what with these silicone chips. Somebody's got their priorities wrong. Then he's always been a right keen smoker, your Dad. Now he's paying the price. (*pause*) Robert Donat had bronchitis. Else it was asthma. He was sensitive, you could tell.

Midgley puts his head in his hands.

AUNTY KITTY	(*indicating a woman in a corner*) Her hubby's on the critical list. Their eldest girl works for Johnson and Johnson. They'd just got back from Barbados.

INTENSIVE CARE

The doctor – an Indian – comes in.

Denis. It's the doctor.

DOCTOR (*looking at his clipboard*) Mr Midgley? Your father has had a stroke. How severe it is hard to tell. However when he was brought in he was suffering from hypothermia. Our old enemy. He must have fallen and been lying there for two days at least.

MIDGLEY I generally go over at weekends.

DOCTOR Pneumonia has now set in. His heart is not strong. I do not think he will last the night.

He puts the clipboard under his arm, and we see there is nothing on it.

15 Hospital Telephone Area

A young man on one telephone.

FAT MAN (*to Midgley, who is also waiting*) Only three phones and two of them duff. You wouldn't credit it. Say you were on standby for a transplant. It'd be all the same.

He jingles his coins.
The young man puts his head out.

YOUNG MAN I've got one or two calls to make.
FAT MAN Oh hell.
ORDERLY There's a phone outside physio. Try there.
FAT MAN I'll try there.
YOUNG MAN Hello, Dorothy? Dorothy, you're a grandma! A grandma. Yes. Well, guess. (*pause*) No. Girl. Seven and a half pounds. At 5.35. Both doing well. I'm ringing everybody. Bye, grandma.

Midgley half rises but the young man makes another call.

Hello, Neil. Hi. You're an uncle. Yes. Just now. 5.35. Well, guess. (*pause*) No, girl. *No*. It's what we really wanted. I think. I'm over the moon. So tell Christine, she's an aunty and yes, a little cousin for Josephine. How's it feel to be an uncle? Bye.

Midgley gets up and stands but the young man, while looking at him, ignores him.

YOUNG MAN Betty? Congratulations. You're an Aunty. I won't ask you

19

to guess. It's a girl. Susan's over the moon. And I am. I'm just telephoning with the glad tidings. Bye, *Aunty*!

MIDGLEY Could I just make one call?
YOUNG MAN Won't it wait? I was here first. I'm a father.
MIDGLEY I'm a son. My father's dying.
YOUNG MAN There's no need to take that tone.

He steps out.

You should have spoken up. There's a phone outside physio.

He waits while Midgley telephones.

MIDGLEY Uncle Ernest. Denis. Dad's been taken poorly. He's had a stroke. And a fall. And now he's got pneumonia. (*The young man looks away abashed*) Can you ring round, tell anybody who might want to come? The doctor says he won't last the night. I'm in a box. There are people waiting.

He puts the telephone down.

YOUNG MAN You never know. They can work miracles nowadays.

16 Outside the Hospital

Ernest is in his seventies.

ERNEST Did you ring our Hartley?

Midgley nods.

Tied up? Secretary, was it?
MIDGLEY He's coming as soon as he can get away.
ERNEST Was he in a meeting? I'd like to know what they are, these meetings he's in that he can't speak to his father. Who are they in these meetings? Don't they have fathers? I thought fathers were universal. Instead of which I have to make an appointment. 'I'll just look at his book.' Sons, fathers, you shouldn't need appointments, you should get straight through. You weren't like that with your Dad. Frank thought the world of you.

17 Hospital

They go into the lift, together with a patient on a trolley with a porter.

ERNEST This is what I'd call an industrial lift.
It's not an ordinary passenger lift, this. It's as big as our sitting room. It'd be a stroke. He's only seventy-two. I'm seventy-four.

The lift stops and a porter gets in with a trolley with a woman on it.

PORTER 2 Is it working?

The little head closes its eyes.

We've just had a nice jab. Had a nice jab and we're going for a ta ta.

ERNEST It was our Hartley that rang. Or rather his secretary. She'll be on five thousand a year. That's a starting salary these days.

They go out into a long corridor.

ERNEST I came on the diesel. It's only one stop. I use my railcard. I go all over. I went to York last week. Saw the railway museum. There's stock in there I drove. Museum in my own lifetime. You still school-teaching?

MIDGLEY Yes.

ERNEST No, I've been all over since your Aunt Edith died. Take a flask. Sandwiches. I plan to visit Barnard Castle next week. Weather permitting.

Outside the Intensive Care Unit Uncle Ernest pauses.

ERNEST Is your Aunty Kitty here?
MIDGLEY Yes.
ERNEST I thought she would be. Where no vultures fly.

Aunty Kitty sees them come in and, as if her grief were too great for words, solemnly embraces her brother, shaking her head and dabbing her nose.

18 Father's Room

Ernest goes alone into father's room.

ERNEST (*awkwardly*) This is summat fresh for you, Frank. You were always such a bouncer.

He looks at the scanner, then sits down again.

I went over to York last week. It's the first time I've been since we used to bike over when we were lads. It hasn't changed much. They haven't spoilt it like they have Leeds. Though there's one of these precinct things. I went on my Railcard. It's still wicked. (*Pause*). I'll say ta ra then, butt. I've come on the diesel. Ta ra.

He jogs his brother's foot in farewell just as the nurse comes in.

NURSE 2 (*reprovingly*) He's very ill. And this is delicate equipment.

19 Hospital Lift

Meanwhile, Hartley, Uncle Ernest's son, Jean, his wife, and two children are coming out of the lift.

HARTLEY Now think on the pair of you, don't be asking for this and that in front of your Grandad.
JEAN Are you listening, Mark? Your father's talking to you. We don't want him saying you're spoiled.
HARTLEY Though you are spoiled.
JEAN Whose fault is that? Mind that nurse, Mark. Sorry.

20 Hospital Corridor

They meet Uncle Ernest coming down the corridor with Midgley.

HARTLEY Look out. Here's your Grandad. Now then, Dad. Denis.
JEAN Grandad. (*She kisses him*) Give your Grandad a kiss, Elizabeth.

The little girl does so.

Mark.
MARK I don't kiss now.
JEAN You kiss your Grandad.

The boy does so shamefacedly.

HARTLEY How is he?
ERNEST Dying. Sinking fast.
HARTLEY Oh dear, oh dear, oh dear.
MIDGLEY They don't think he'll last the night.
JEAN How've you been keeping?
MIDGLEY Champion.

HARTLEY	I had the receiver in my hand to give you a ring, yesterday, Dad, only a client came in.
ERNEST	That one of them new watches?
MARK	Yes.
JEAN	He had it to save up for. You had it to save up for didn't you, Mark?
ELIZABETH	He didn't.
ERNEST	I didn't have a watch till I was twenty-one. 'Course they're twenty-one at eighteen now, aren't they.
HARTLEY	We'd better be getting along to the ward if it's that critical.
JEAN	Shall we see you soon, Grandad?
ERNEST	I was thinking of going to Barnard Castle next week.
JEAN	Whatever for?
ERNEST	I've never been.
HARTLEY	Say goodbye then.
JEAN	Kiss your Grandad.

The children kiss him again.

MIDGLEY	I'll just see you to the lift.

Hartley and Jean and their children go along the corridor.

JEAN	I'll give you such a clatter when I get you home, young lady. He did save up.
ELIZABETH	Only a week.
HARTLEY	Now when we get there we shan't have to go in all at once. It'll just be two at a time.
JEAN	What's he doing going to Barnard Castle? He can't be short of money taking himself off to Barnard Castle.

21 Father's Room

Hartley and Mark go into Father's room.

HARTLEY	Hello, Uncle. It's Hartley. There's Mark too. We're all here.

They stand awkwardly waiting. Hartley's attention is increasingly caught by the television monitor. The boy looks distastefully at the bed.

HARTLEY	You see this screen, Mark. It's monitoring his heart beats.
MARK	(*witheringly*) I know, Dad.

HARTLEY I was only telling you.
MARK (*as they go out*) I've made one of those at school.

Elizabeth and Jean come in.

ELIZABETH Are you crying Mam?
JEAN Yes.
ELIZABETH There aren't many tears.
JEAN You can cry without tears.
ELIZABETH I can't. How do you do it, Mam?
JEAN I'll give you such a smack in a minute, your Uncle Denis's father is dying.

Elizabeth starts to cry.

JEAN There, love. It's all right. He doesn't feel it.
ELIZABETH I'm not crying because of him. I'm crying because of you.

22 Waiting Room

Back in the waiting room, Midgley and Hartley are sitting opposite an Indian father who is weeping and hugging his son tightly to him.

HARTLEY I wouldn't have another Cortina. I used to swear by Cortinas.

Midgley looks at the Indian family.

You still got the VW?

Midgley nods.

I might go in for a Peugeot next. A 604. Buy British.

Jean and Elizabeth return.

JEAN How long are we stopping?
HARTLEY I think we ought to wait just a bit, don't you, darling?
JEAN Oh yes. Just in case.
HARTLEY He was a nice old chap.

Aunty Kitty comes in.

AUNTY KITTY I just had one coffee and a wagonwheel and it was forty-five pence. And it's all supposed to be voluntary.
MARK There isn't a disco, is there?
JEAN Disco? Disco? This is a hospital.
MARK Leisure facilities. Facilities for visitors. Killing time.

JEAN Listen. Your Uncle Denis's father is dying and you talk about discos.
MIDGLEY It's all right.
HARTLEY Here. (*handing him a pound*) Go get yourself a coffee.

23 Hospital Corridor. Evening

A woman on sticks hobbles painfully along a corridor to a radiator.

WOMAN (*to no one in particular*) I do love chrysanths.
HARTLEY You want to make it plain at this stage you don't want him resuscitating.
JEAN That is if he doesn't want him resuscitating.
HARTLEY I wouldn't.
JEAN Denis might. You don't know.

Midgley looks as if he doesn't know either.

HARTLEY You often don't get the choice. They'll resuscitate anybody given half a chance. You read about it. Shove them on these life support machines. It's all to do with cost effectiveness. They invest in this expensive equipment and then of course they have to use it.
JEAN Miracles do happen, of course. I was reading about these out of body experiences. Have you read about them, Denis? Out of body experiences. Where sick people float in the air above their own bodies. I think it won't be long before science will be coming round to an afterlife. Bye bye.

Hartley's family exits.

WOMAN (*again, to no one in particular*) They've put me down for one of these electric chair things. Once I get one of them I shall be whizzing about all over.

The Indian father and the little boy are now both asleep.

UNTY KITTY Money's no good. Look at President Kennedy. They've been a tragic family. (*pause*) The Wainwrights got back from Corfu. They said they enjoyed it but they wouldn't go again. (*pause*) If I go now I can just get the twenty to.
MIDGLEY I'll come down and phone Joyce.

They tiptoe past the sleeping Indians.

AUNTY KITTY The little lad's bonny. They've got feelings the same as us. They're fond of their families. More so probably, because they're less advanced than we are.

24 Telephone Area

In the telephone area. While Kitty goes towards the exit, Midgley is phoning.

MIDGLEY I've got to be here.

25 Midgley's Home

Mrs Midgley's mother asleep, his son watching television, and Mrs Midgley on the telephone.

MRS MIDGLEY You've done all that's necessary. Nobody would blame you.

26 Telephone Area

MIDGLEY I've got to be here. I must be here when he goes. Can't you understand that?

27 Midgley's Home

MRS MIDGLEY I understand you. It's not love. It's not affection. It's yourself.

She puts the telephone down.

COLIN Dad?
MRS MIDGLEY He's hanging on.
COLIN Who?
MRS MIDGLEY Your *Grandad*. Wake up, Mum. Time for bed.

28 Hospital Room

In the Intensive Care room, Midgley is sitting by the bed. The night nurse, Valery, comes in and does jobs round the bed.

MIDGLEY Am I in the way?
VALERY No. Stop there.

He watches her. She is less pert than the others, more sloppy. She smiles at him and goes out.
Later, she looks in again.

VALERY Cup of tea?

Midgley nods.
Later.

VALERY Slack tonight. Touch wood. It just takes one drunken driver. Still. It's not dull.

Midgley is dropping asleep.

I thought you were going to be a bit of company. You're tired out. Lie down.

She gives him a pillow and they go out to the waiting room.

VALERY I'll give you a shout if anything happens.

The Indians are also asleep.

29 Hospital Waiting Room

Next morning, in the waiting room, Midgley is being shaken awake by the day nurse.

NURSE 3 Excuse me, excuse me. You can't lie down. You're not supposed to lie down.

Midgley sits up.
The Indians have gone and in their place two anonymous people are staring at him expressionlessly.

MIDGLEY The nurse said she'd wake me up.
NURSE 3 What nurse
MIDGLEY If anything happened to my father.
NURSE 3 Which is your father?
MIDGLEY Midgley.
NURSE 3 Is that a hospital pillow?
MIDGLEY Mr Midgley.
NURSE 3 No. No change. But don't lie down. It's not fair on other people.

30 Father's Room

Midgley goes into his father's room. While he looks rough and unshaven, his father looks pink and clean and fresh.

31 Car Park

Midgley goes out to his van in the car park, and looks at himself in the car mirror, then gets out and walks round the outside of the hospital.
He sees a woman at a window suckling a baby, then sees a nurse appear behind her.
He walks on, finds himself outside Intensive Care, and looks up at his father's room. He sees a nurse with her back to the window, and then another nurse comes in.
The room seems full of people.
He begins to scramble down the bank to try and get into this section of the building, tries a door, but it's locked. He tries another door, then scrambles on through some bushes, across a muddy flowerbed, and finally finds himself at the main entrance.

32 Father's Room

He rushes past the desk into his father's room.

MIDGLEY Is he dead?

The nurses look round.

MATRON Dead? Certainly not. I am the matron. Look at your shoes.

As the nurses bustle Midgley out he looks back and we get a glimpse of his father's face: he could be smiling.

MIDGLEY But I want to see a doctor.
MATRON Why? Have you a complaint?
MIDGLEY The doctor yesterday said my father wouldn't last the night. He has, so I was wondering if there was any change.
MATRON No change. I should go home. You've done your duty.

33 Waiting Room

Back in the waiting room, Aunty Kitty has got her knitting, a flask, biscuits, and is quite settled in.
The Indians are back waiting too.

AUNTY KITTY (*to someone else waiting*) I've just been to spend a penny. When you consider it's a hospital, the toilets are nothing to write home about.

She is immersed in the magazine Country Life.

I know one thing. I shouldn't thank you for a house in Bermuda. Where've you been with your shoes?

Midgley looks at his muddy shoes.

And you'd better ring your Uncle Ernest. He'll want the latest gen.

34 Toilet

Midgley goes into the gents toilet, gets some toilet paper and cleans the mud off his boots.
He has put his shoes on again and is standing with the muddy toilet paper when an orderly comes in, looks at him and the paper with incredulity and disgust, and goes into a cubicle shaking his head.

ORDERLY The bastard public. The nasty, dirty, bastard public.

Midgley looks at the paper and puts it in the bin.

35 Telephone Area

Midgley is patiently waiting, while a woman is on the telephone.

WOMAN Cyril. It's Vi. Mam's had her op. Had it this morning first thing. She's not come round yet but apparently she's fine. Yes, fine. I spoke to the sister and she says it wasn't what they thought it was, so there's no need to worry. I don't know what it was, she did tell me the name, but the important thing is that it wasn't what they thought it was. No. Completely clear. The sister would know, wouldn't she? Oh yes, I think it's good news, and she said the surgeon is the best. People pay thousands to have him she said. Anyway I'll see you later. I'm so relieved. Aren't you? Yes. Bye.

36 Father's Room

ERNEST Jillo, Frank. We can't go on like this, you know. I can't run to the fares.

37 Waiting Room

Uncle Ernest goes to the waiting room.

AUNTY KITTY It's Frank all over. Going down fighting. He loved life. He won't go without a struggle ... it's their daughter ...

She indicates an elderly couple waiting.

Just choosing some new curtains in Schofields. Collapsed. Suspected brain haemorrhage. Their other son's a vet.

38 Hospital Corridor

ERNEST (*as they walk along the corridor*) It's a wonder to me how your Aunty Kitty's managed to escape strangulation so long. Was he coloured, this doctor?
MIDGLEY Who?
ERNEST That said he was on his last legs.
MIDGLEY Yes.
ERNEST That explains it.
HARTLEY Dad.
ERNEST What do you mean 'Dad'?
HARTLEY I mean I'm vice chairman of the community relations council, that's what I mean. I mean we've got one in the office and he's a tip top accountant. We all have to live with one another in this world.
ERNEST You're young.
ERNEST I'll not come again. It starts out of respect. Only it gets morbid. I'd go back home if I were you.

Midgley says nothing.

HARTLEY We've got to play it by ear.
ERNEST There's no need to go through all this performance with me, you know. Come once and have done. Mind you, I'll be lucky if you come at all.
HARTLEY Shall I drop you?
ERNEST I don't want you to go out of your way.
HARTLEY No, but shall I drop you?

Midgley watches them disappear into the lift, still arguing, and then he walks back along the corridor. A woman on sticks passes him.

WOMAN I'm getting one of these mobile trolley things. Once I get that I'll be up and down this corridor.

39 Father's Room

Next evening, as he waits in his father's room, Valery, the night nurse, comes in with a bowl and a sponge.

VALERY He doesn't want to leave us, does he?

Midgley goes and looks out of the window as she washes him.

I can see his attraction even though he's old. I can imagine women going for him.
MIDGLEY (*uncomfortably*) Women didn't go for him. Only my mother.
VALERY I don't believe that.

Midgley turns just as she is sponging between his father's legs. He turns back hastily.

What was he?
MIDGLEY What do you mean?
VALERY What was his job?
MIDGLEY Plumber.
VALERY What are you?
MIDGLEY Teacher.
VALERY He's got lovely hands. Real ladies hands. You see that happen in hospitals. People's hands change.

Midgley turns and she is holding his father's hand.

40 Night Nurse's Desk. Later

A very young doctor sits there.

DOCTOR There hasn't been any particular change. His condition certainly hasn't deteriorated. On the other hand it hasn't improved.
MIDGLEY The other doctor said he wouldn't last the night.
DOCTOR I don't know there's any special point in waiting. You've done your duty.
MIDGLEY I don't think he is dying.
DOCTOR Living, dying. (*shrugs slightly*) There's nothing special about the moment of death. The screen will alter, that's all. You do *want* your father to live, Mr Midgley?
MIDGLEY Yes, only I was told he wasn't going to last long.
DOCTOR Our task is to make them last as long as possible. We've no obligation to get them off on time. This isn't British Rail.

MIDGLEY Look, how old are you?

The doctor turns away, pulls a small face at Valery and goes.

MIDGLEY I don't like fifteen year old doctors, that's all. I'm old enough to be his father.
VALERY Why not go and sleep in your van. If anything happens I'll send somebody down.
MIDGLEY Does nobody else wait? Does nobody else feel like me? (*pause*) What do you do during the day, when you're on nights?
VALERY Sleep. I generally surface around three.
MIDGLEY Maybe we could have a coffee? If he's unchanged.
VALERY O.K.
MIDGLEY I'll just have another squint then I'll go.

41 Father's Room

He goes into his father's room, and then returns, quickly.

MIDGLEY Come look. He's moved.

They go back in together.

VALERY No.
MIDGLEY Yes.

She switches on the overhead light.

MIDGLEY He's kind of smiling.
VALERY No.
MIDGLEY If you look long enough you'll see.
VALERY If you long enough you'll see anything you want. You're tired. Goodnight.

Midgley would probably kiss her, were his father not present.

42 Midgley's Home

Cut to Mrs Midgley on the telephone.
Her mother is sitting with her bag by the sitting room door.

MRS MIDGLEY Sit down a minute, Mother. I'll be with you in a minute. Mum's waiting to go up. She's crying out for a bath. I'm just steeling myself. What do you do all day?

43 Telephone Area

Cut to Midgley on the telephone.

MIDGLEY I need a bath.

MRS MIDGLEY Go over to your Dad's. It's not all that far. If it's not going to be any minute you might as well. I'm going to have to go.

Her mother nearly falls off the chair, but she stops her in time.

MOTHER What am I doing sitting on this chair? I never sit on this chair. I don't think I've ever sat on this chair before.

44 Midgley's Car

Next morning. Valery bangs on Midgley's car window.

VALERY *(mouthing)* Just coming off.

Midgley winds the window down.

Isn't it a grand morning I'm just coming off. I'm going to have a big breakfast then go to bed. I'll see you at teatime. You look terrible.

Midgley sees his face in the driving mirror: he does.
She walks off and he starts up the van and drives after her.

MIDGLEY I forgot to ask you. How's my Dad?
VALERY No change.

She waves and runs down towards the nurses' flats.

No change.

45 Midgley's Father's House

Midgley drives to his father's terrace house in a street in Leeds. Inside it is neat and silent. There are photographs of father and mother, of a wedding and photographs of grandchildren.

Midgley goes into the scullery and pours water from kettle into a bowl. He looks at his father's razor, cleans it, changes the blade, and find his father's old shaving brush which is worn down to a stub. When he has finished shaving he wipes his face on the towel on the back of the door. Then he takes his shirt off, washes, and smells his shirt. Then he goes upstairs to his parents' bedroom.

INTENSIVE CARE

This room is neat too, with brushes and a mirror laid out on the glass dressing table. He looks in a drawer, and finds a new shirt which is still in Christmas paper. He puts it on: it's too big. He looks at socks and underpants, and then he dresses.

When he has finished he goes down to the sitting room and stands by the fireplace. He looks as if he's ready for a funeral.
His father's pipe is on the mantelpiece. He looks at it, then puts it back. It falls to the hearth. He stops to pick it up, then suddenly thinks of his father doing the same, falling and lying there.

Suddenly, thinking of his father dead, he panics and rushes out of the house, and drives away very quickly.

46 Father's Room, Hospital

MIDGLEY I'm wearing your shirt, Dad. It's the one we gave you for Christmas. I hope that's all right. It doesn't really suit me but I think that's why Joyce bought it. She said it didn't suit me so it would suit you.

The day nurse comes in, and raises her eyebrows, indicating she thinks he is mad, talking to his father like this.

They tell you to talk. I read it in Readers Digest. It was in the waiting room.

NURSE 3 They say the same thing about plants. I think it's got past that stage.

47 Valery's Room

In Valery's room in the nurses' home, Midgley and Valery have just had tea.

VALERY People are funny about nurses. Men. You say you're a nurse and their whole attitude changes. Do you know what I mean?
MIDGLEY No.
VALERY I've noticed it at parties. They ask you what you do, you say you're a nurse, and next minute they're behaving like animals. Perfectly ordinary people. They turn into wild beasts. I've given up saying I'm a nurse for that reason.
MIDGLEY What do you say you are, medieval historian?

VALERY No. I say I'm a personal secretary. But that's why I liked you. You're obviously not like that.

Midgley is silent.

Of course you've got other things on your mind.

MIDGLEY What?
VALERY He is lovely. Your Dad. I do understand the way you feel about him. Old people have their own particular attraction I think. He does anyway.

Midgley can't relax.

Was your cake gritty?
MIDGLEY No.
VALERY Mine was. Mine was a bit gritty.
MIDGLEY It was probably meant to be gritty.
VALERY No. It was more gritty than that.

Silence.

MIDGLEY What would you say if I asked you to go to bed?
VALERY I suppose it's with you being a nurse they think you've seen everything. When? Now?
MIDGLEY Yes.
VALERY I can't now.
MIDGLEY Why not? You're not on till seven.
VALERY No. It's Wednesday. I'm on early turn.
MIDGLEY Tomorrow then.
VALERY Tomorrow would be better. Though of course it all depends.
MIDGLEY What on?
VALERY Your father. He may not be here tomorrow.
MIDGLEY No. I'd better go back then.
VALERY Fingers crossed.

48 Father's Room

MIDGLEY Hold on, Dad. Hold on.

49 Telephone Area

Midgley is calling home.

MIDGLEY Colin. It's Dad. Is your Mam there?

50 Midgley's Home

COLIN She's upstairs with Gran. Mum. Dad wants you.
MRS MIDGLEY (*shouting*) I can't. I'm bathing your Grandma. I can't leave her.
COLIN She says she can't leave her.

51 Telephone Area

MIDGLEY You go up and watch her. I want to speak to your Mam.

52 Midgley's Home

COLIN Dad, she's in the bath. She's no clothes on. Dad, I won't.

Mrs Midgley puts her head round the bathroom door.

MRS MIDGLEY Tell him if I can get a granny sitter I'm going to come over.
COLIN She says she's going to come over.

53 Telephone Area

MIDGLEY No. Don't do that. Tell her not to do that. There's no need. Are you there? Go on, tell her.

54 Midgley's Home

COLIN I'll tell her.

55 Telephone Area

MIDGLEY You won't. You'll forget. Go up and tell her now.
He waits.

56 Midgley's Home

COLIN Mum. Dad says there's no need.
MRS MIDGLEY No need to what?
COLIN Go over.

57 Telephone Area

MIDGLEY Did you tell her? Good. Haven't you forgotten something? 'How's Grandad, Dad? Is he any better?' 'Nice of you to ask, Colin. He's about the same, thank you.'

58 Midgley's Home

Colin putting the telephone down wearily, as Mrs Midgley comes in with a wet towel and a bundle of underclothes.

MRS MIDGLEY How was your Grandad?
COLIN About the same.
MRS MIDGLEY And your Dad?
COLIN No change.

59 Hospital Car Park

Midgley is asleep in his van. Someone else gets in.

MIDGLEY Who's that?
HIS FATHER Only me.
MIDGLEY Hello Dad.
FATHER I thought we'd go for a drive.

They drive off.

MIDGLEY When did you learn to drive?
FATHER Just before I died.
MIDGLEY I never knew that.
FATHER There's lots of things you don't know.

60 Midgley's Van

As they drive along the scene changes dramatically and inexplicably from town to country, from back streets to palaces.

FATHER Isn't that your Mam when she was younger?

He stops the van and a pretty woman gets in.

Mam.

MOTHER Hello Dad. Hello Denis. What a spanking van.
FATHER Move over, Denis.

Midgley suddenly becomes a small boy.

Let your Mam sit next to me.

They sit in a row and Midgley sees his Dad's hand on his mother's knee.

61 Field

Then Midgley as a boy is sitting with his mother in a field.

MOTHER This field is spotless. It's a lovely field. We can sit here all day. Just the two of us.

He turns round and sees a huge slag heap at the edge of the field: he is horrified. His mother carries on, oblivious.

Aren't you glad we brought a flask?

A man, covered in grime, runs down the slag heap: it is his father. His mother is in white.

BOY (*in terror*) Mam! Mam!

She looks round.

MOTHER It's only your Dad, love.

She smiles and he sits down beside her, his black hand on her white frock.

62 Leeds Market

Next, Midgley, and his mother and father (now old) are walking through Leeds market. The place is empty, the stalls shuttered and closed.

63 Motorway

Next they are driving along a motorway. The turnoffs are marked with the names of places like Leeds, Barnsley, Sheffield. Then they change to Heart Disease, Cancer.

64 Hospital Reception Area

Next his mother and father are sitting in the reception area of that hospital, but it is also some kind of station. They kiss, and look round, but Midgley is not there.

Above their heads there is a station noticeboard, but instead of arrivals and departures it says 'births' and 'deaths' and keeps clicking over with different names. She kisses his father goodbye and goes through the gates, just as Midgley comes up. He shakes the gates shouting 'Mam, Mam.' But she has gone. He turns round and looks at his father who is shaking his head, obviously disappointed with him.
Midgley shakes the gates again calling 'Mam, Mam' as it changes to Valery knocking on the window of the van to wake him.
She waves and goes off towards her quarters.

Later that day, a smart car draws up, driven by a woman, elegantly dressed in her late fifties. She gets out and walks towards the hospital. When Midgley comes into his father's room, she is sitting there, holding his father's hand, quite unruffled.

ALICE   Is it Denis?
MIDGLEY   Yes.
ALICE   I'm Alice Duckworth. Did he tell you about me?
MIDGLEY   No.
ALICE   No. He wouldn't. The old bugger. He told me about you. It's a sad sight. Though that slut of a nurse says he's a bit better this morning. His condition's stabilised, whatever that means. Shouldn't think she knows. You look a bit scruffy. I've come from Southport.

She gets up and puts the carnations in the bin.

Carnations are depressing flowers.

She replaces them with flowers she has brought herself.

I'm a widow. A rich widow. Shall we have a meander round? No sense in stopping here. His lordship's not got much to contribute.

She and Midgley go out into the reception area, where they get themselves some coffee.

ALICE   (*taking out a flask from her bag*) Do you want a drop of this in it?
MIDGLEY   No thanks.
ALICE   I'd better. I've driven from Southport. I wanted to marry your Dad, did you know that? He said no. Why? Because I'd got too much money. My husband left me very nicely placed; he was a leading light in the soft furnishing trade.

INTENSIVE CARE

He'd have felt beholden, you see. That was your Dad all over. Couldn't bear to be under an obligation. Still you know what he was like.

MIDGLEY He was good. Everybody says how good he was.

ALICE He always had to be the one, did Frank. The one who did the good turns, the one who paid out, the one who sacrificed. You couldn't do anything for him. I had all this money, he wouldn't even let me take him to Scarborough. We used to go sit in Roundhay Park. Roundhay Park! We could have been in Tenerife. (*she blows her nose*) Still, I'd have put up with that.

MIDGLEY That's why I've been waiting. That's why I wanted to be here. I didn't want to let him down. And he wants me to let him down, I know.

The woman on crutches goes past.

ALICE What was your Mam like?
MIDGLEY She was lovely.
ALICE She must have had him taped. She looks a grand woman. He's showed me photographs. (*she makes up*) Any road, I'll go and have another look at him. Then I've got to get over to a Round Table in Harrogate. Killed two birds with one stone for me, this trip.

MIDGLEY You don't know. If he comes round he might reconsider your offer.

She looks at Midgley and smiles, then gives him a kiss.

ALICE And don't you be like you Dad, think on. You go your own way.

65 Waiting Room. Later

AUNT KITTY Your Mother'd not been dead a year. I was shocked.
MIDGLEY I'm not shocked.
AUNT KITTY You're a man. It wasn't like your Dad. She's got a cheek showing her face.
MIDGLEY I'm rather pleased.
AUNT KITTY And her hair's dyed. A real common woman. Anyway they're sending him downstairs tomorrow. He must be on the mend. I hope when he does come round he's not a vegetable. Where are you going?
MIDGLEY I said I'd see someone.

66 Valery's Flat

Midgley is in the bathroom brushing his teeth.

VALERY Maureen knows to ring if anything happens. Not that it will. His chest is better. His heart is better. He's simply unconscious now. I'm looking forward to him coming round. I long to know what his voice is like.

Midgley turns the tap off.

MIDGLEY What?
VALERY I long to know what his voice is like.
MIDGLEY Oh. Yes.

He turns the tap on again.

VALERY I think I know. I'd just like to have it confirmed.

Midgley comes into the bedroom.

You don't like talking about your Father, do you? (*she is undressing*) Nice shirt.

MIDGLEY Yes. One of Dad's.
VALERY Nice.

He goes to the bathroom and she takes the telephone off the hook. Midgley gets into bed; she is already there.

MIDGLEY Hello. (*Pause*) It's a bit daft, is this.
VALERY Why? It happens all the time.
MIDGLEY It's what people call living, is this. We're living. (*they kiss*) I ought to have done more of this.
VALERY What?
MIDGLEY Living. This is going to be the rule from now on. I've got a lot of catching up to do. It's the nick of time.
VALERY I've never heard it called that.
MIDGLEY Dirty bugger.
VALERY You started it. 'What would you say if I said could we go to bed?' I mean.
MIDGLEY That's technique, that is. It avoids direct confrontation.
VALERY I think I could do with some confrontation.
MIDGLEY You've done this before. I hope this isn't one of those private beds. It's not BUPA is it, this? Otherwise I may have to leave. I'm opposed to that on principle.
VALERY People do talk rubbish in bed.

MIDGLEY Only place left. Only place where you can act daft. Not what we do. Me and Joyce. If Joyce ever does anything fresh I know it's because she's been reading in a magazine that she ought to.
VALERY You never asked me if I was married.
MIDGLEY You're a nurse. You're above marriage. (*pause*) Are you married?
VALERY He's on an oil rig.
MIDGLEY I bloody hope so.

Afterwards

MIDGLEY I feel better after that. Nurse. (*pause*) I was certain they were going to ring.
VALERY (*smiling*) No.

She puts the receiver back on. He looks a bit shocked, then shrugs.

MIDGLEY (*grinning*) No harm done. Still, I suppose I ought to be getting back.
VALERY We've still got half an hour.
MIDGLEY Yes?

They are just settling down again when the phone rings.

VALERY Yes? Yes.

She is looking at Midgley as she is speaking.

VALERY You'd better go.
MIDGLEY What's matter?
VALERY Go.
MIDGLEY Had she been trying before?
VALERY You'd better go.
MIDGLEY (*frantic*) Had she been trying?
VALERY *Go.*

67 Father's Room

Aunty Kitty, Mrs Midgley, and Midgley are all there.

AUNTY KITTY It's the biggest wonder I hadn't popped in to see Mrs Tunnicliffe. She's over in Ward 7 having a plastic hip, she's been waiting two years, but I don't know what it was, something made me come back upstairs and I was

	sat looking at some reading matter when in walks Joyce and we'd hardly had time to say hello when the nurse comes running out to say he had his eyes open. So we were both there, weren't we, Joyce?
MRS MIDGLEY	He just said 'Is our Denis here?'
AUNT KITTY	And I said 'He's coming, Frank. It's me, Kitty.' And he just smiled and it was all over. It was a beautiful way to go. I'm glad I was here to see it. I was his only sister. (*pause*) The dots do something different when you're dying. I wasn't watching it naturally, but out of the corner of my eye I noticed it was doing something different during his last moments.
MRS MIDGLEY	He's smiling.

The body lies on the bed, sheet up to the neck.

MIDGLEY	Of course he's smiling. He's won. He's scored. In the last minute of extra time.

Mrs Midgley looks disgusted, and goes out. Porters appear to transfer the body to a trolley.

AUNTY KITTY	It's a pity you weren't here, Denis. You've been here all the time he was dying. What were you doing?
MIDGLEY	Living.
AUNTY KITTY	He just said 'Is our Denis here?' then smiled that little smile and it was all over.

68 Hospital Room

At a counter, a hospital administrator, going through a form, with Dad's folded clothes in front of him.

ADMIN'TOR	One gunmetal watch. Wallet with senior citizen's bus pass. Seventy four and a half pence in change. One doorkey.

He pushes the form over for Midgley to sign.

MIDGLEY	Have you something I can put them in?
ADMIN'TOR	They never bring bags. It's not our job, you know, bags.

In the wallet there is a photograph of Midgley and his mother, when younger, laughing together.
He looks at this while the man roots about for a bag.

INTENSIVE CARE

69 Midgley's Home

That evening in Midgley's kitchen.
Midgley and Mrs Midgley are sitting in their overcoats.

MRS MIDGLEY You didn't let him down. You went for a walk. That's not letting him down.
MIDGLEY I wasn't there.

Colin comes in with a girlfriend.

COLIN Hello Dad. Long time no see.

Midgley doesn't respond.

Did Grandad die?
MRS MIDGLEY This afternoon.
COLIN Oh. Jane's just going to have some coffee.
MRS MIDGLEY Take her in the other room.

They go out.

(*calling*) Put the fire on.

She pours out the coffee.

A short while later, Midgley happens to pass the sitting room and, seeing the door ajar, pushes it open.
Colin is kissing the girl.

MIDGLEY (*after watching for a moment*) We've just lost your Grandad. You might show some feeling.

Mrs Midgley appears behind him as Midgley goes.

MRS MIDGLEY Take no notice. He's upset. There's nothing to be ashamed of. It's only your father.

She smiles sweetly.

70 School Office. Next Day

Miss Tunstall is typing.

MISS T Well, at least he didn't suffer.
MIDGLEY Oh no.

She stops and reaches for her cigarettes.

MISS T   When my mother finally pulls her socks up and dies I'm going to go on a world cruise.
MIDGLEY   (*reaching for a cigarette*) May I?
MISS T   I didn't know you smoked.
MIDGLEY   I thought I might start.
MISS T   Bit late in the day.
MIDGLEY   What's this?

He reaches over and takes the notice she is copying.

MISS T   It's one of his 'privilege not a right' notices.
MIDGLEY   (*reading*) 'Pupils are reminded that coming to school in their own cars is a privilege, not a right. There have been several unsavoury incidents recently ...' I like 'unsavoury'. '... of pupils resorting to their cars in the lunch hour to indulge in sexual intercourse.'

Miss Tunstall hurriedly retrieves the notice to check this is just Midgley's joke.

MISS T   'Immoral behaviour.'
MIDGLEY   'Immoral behaviour.' Where are you going to go on this world cruise?

Miss Tunstall shrugs and starts typing again.

MISS T   Bridlington, I expect.

Midgley, in his overcoat and carrying his briefcase, walks away down the long corridor, past a small boy looking out of the window.

The Flip Side of Dominick Hide

by Jeremy Paul and Alan Gibson

An Introduction by Alan Gibson

The seeds for Dominick Hide were sown in the summer of 1953. I was at a farewell party at my uncle's house in Toronto: my family and I were travelling the next day to holiday in England. I was just fifteen and very excited.

People were discussing some recent newspaper reports of 'UFO's' – Unidentified Flying Objects, as they were then called. It was all very mysterious: there seemed to be a veil of secrecy over the whole thing, yet the people who claimed to have sighted these flying objects (always for some reason saucer-shaped) were described as being everyday folk. My uncle was convinced that they were spy planes from Russia, checking us out and monitoring the Western World. Someone else said they were aliens from outer space, with a strange luminosity and flying too fast to be anything from our planet. There had in fact been one sighting by a USAF pilot who had chased a UFO in his jet and found that it simply disappeared.

Suddenly I heard myself saying to my uncle and the other adults that the answer seemed obvious. Since there had been sightings of flying saucers recorded throughout history, it occurred to me that they were man-made machines, time machines from the future when mankind had solved the problem of time-travel. I was half joking, but with the arrogance of youth I continued to expound my theory. To my surprise, my idea was received with genuine interest.

In those days people usually crossed the Atlantic by boat, and our journey to England took eight days. But the return journey was by aeroplane with a refuelling stop in Iceland. I loved flying then. The propeller planes never went so high that you couldn't see some activity on the ground, or at least imagine that you could observe the bustling community below. Over the ocean there was no idea of height until you'd occasionally see the tiny white dart of a ship's wake breaking the slate grey of the sea and then you'd wonder at the commanding view you had of the world. You were part of the earth, yet at one remove.

As I gazed out of the tiny window I thought again of my absurd, but logical idea of a future government department of social historians with a pool of flying saucers and pilots able to travel backwards in time to any era, and the idea began to grow into a story. But it was to be twenty years before I did anything more about it.

By this time, I was a freelance TV director, married with two daughters, very busy and with little time for writing plays. However, I did write a treatment, just a few pages on the story, and called it *The Flip Side of Dominick Hide*, the flipside being the time before the breaking of the Time Barrier.

Why the flip side? During the fifties in Canada I had often discovered that the B-side of a pop record was a catchier, better song than the A-side (the hit side). The flip side was something you didn't know much about until you got your record home. Sometimes it would be a disappointment, but sometimes a sweet surprise, but it was always an intriguing mystery till you played it. The hero's name came purely out of the rhythm of the phrase, to go with flip side.

So with my rough story and my title, I sent the idea out into the television marketplace. After four years of rejections and then a gap while it sat on the shelf I finally submitted it directly to Keith Williams, the new Head of Plays, at the BBC.

To my delight and astonishment he asked me when I could deliver a first draft of the full script! He would like to fit it into the Play for Today slot in the next season. My delight then gave way to panic. Although I had lived with the story, the characters, the imagery (Dominick's dark suit and deacon's hat had been the subject of many a doodle over many years) I had never written anything before. So this is where Jeremy Paul enters the picture. I had directed two plays he had written several years before. I liked his quirky humour with its tenderness and naivety. I asked if he was interested in collaborating. After several meetings and pints I convinced him that Dominick's story wasn't only science fiction but also a love story. A search for roots, a yearning for security in all of us today and in all of us in the future. A taste of immortality. The future in Dominick Hide's world isn't bad at all. There's still love and music and babies. Family and friends and home. Things to cherish, things to be comfortable with. We wanted to create a concept of the future which differed from the more usual doom-laden. A concept where you could feel nostalgia for something you hadn't yet experienced, a nostalgia for the future. That's perhaps why the play touched so many people.

Alan Gibson, June 1987

Alan Gibson died on July 5th, 1987, at the age of forty-nine. *The Flip Side of Dominick Hide*, with its humour and optimism, and its theme of rebirth and eternal youth, is the very best kind of memorial to him. *Ed.*

An Introduction by Jeremy Paul

My main worry, when Alan first approached me with the idea, was that I don't know the first thing about the internal combustion engine, let alone the interior workings of a flying saucer. Technology in all forms scares me, and in dramatic form tends to bore me. I've never been interested in intergalactic goings-on, except as a purely visual wonderland, as in moments in Space Odyssey. I felt deeply unqualified to write his dream, but as he persisted I began to see what he was after. The fact is, *nobody* actually knows how to describe future time travel, which means that *anybody* is free to invent more or less anything they like. Just note how Dominick and Alaric deal with the routine landing procedure. It's complete nonsense. Or – is it? Who can be sure?

So once I'd got over the science fiction worry, I suddenly started to relax. I'd always liked the concept of Dominick. By chance, Dominick is my father's name. I didn't know my father well, so Dominick's search for his roots, his lost past, became very appealing to me. I was on board.

Collaboration is a mysterious business. You may wonder who actually writes what bit, and wouldn't two writers be constantly arguing about his line or mine? And, of course, although we may agree on the general shape of the story, we may have very different opinions on specific moments and characters, and their precise relationship with each other. Well, the truth is that when the collaboration is good, you forget how it was done. I can't remember any serious disagreements, though there must have been some, and I certainly can't remember who thought up, say, the moment when Dominick collides with the real guitarist in the restaurant, mistaking him for a hologram.

Perhaps it worked because we weren't in competition

with each other. I didn't have a burning desire to direct it (too much hard work) and Alan, although it was his idea, didn't actually want the chore of putting the words down (too much hard work). Alan has a wonderful and wittily visual way of seeing things. He was already directing an unwritten play ... in his head. Like those days when you can successfully capture and describe a dream, vividly and accurately, in all its colours, but the words aren't quite there.

We took an empty office on the top floor of the East Tower at the BBC Television Centre. It gave us a panoramic view of a particularly sprawling and drab piece of West London — we seemed to be hovering in Dominick's saucer. From the window we saw a large advertising board with the name 'Henry Boot' on it, so he became Harry Shoe, the owner of the fair. We saw the rain, the bus queues, three 88 buses arriving at once ... the sheer disorganisation of our life and landscape, the waste of space and resources. And Dominick sensing that somewhere in the mess, his own great-great-grandfather was alive. Can you imagine if we had that opportunity to gaze down at London in the eighteenth century? No wonder Dominick had to land.

But first we had to decide where Dominick had come from. What life would be like in London, one hundred and fifty years from now. And here the fun really began. Did you know cricket will be flourishing? And Scrabble? And tea still drunk? And one of the C's will have fallen out of Piccadilly on the underground which is now called the Bullet? And you can get from Rotherhithe to Rayners Lane on the Bullet in nine seconds? Imagine the difference in the quality of life if there was no rush hour. If stress had largely been eradicated from our lives. If social injustice had really been resolved by the advance of technology. If domestic life and kitchen chores had been more or less eliminated. Would everyone be happier? Or do we perhaps need difficulties, a constant flow of challenges, to stimulate us into getting up in the morning and function at our best? What would we do with all the extra time on our hands? Note how quickly Ava can produce supper from tablets, but note also that the old-fashioned mouthwatering look of the roast beef is preserved.

AN INTRODUCTION BY JEREMY PAUL

We made the assumption that order has been achieved, which means that somehow the problems of the world's economy will have been resolved. We speak of no nuclear catastrophe, although we allude to a mysterious and unpleasant event in 1999, as predicted by the 16th century French astrologer, Nostradamus. We question what happens, in what we might term a complacent society, to culture and to entertainment. It could be a barren time for art and theatre and music, if one believes that great art can only be produced out of conflict and social disorder. It may be no surprise that Dominick has a nostalgic yearning for the Beatles.

And what will happen to language in this homogenized world? If emotions have been largely controlled by science, extremes of language may disappear. People may no longer find themselves 'over the moon' or 'sick as a parrot', but merely pleased or mildly disappointed. The word 'happy' even seems too strong for Alaric. He prefers 'complacent'. And when Ida wins the pool game, he exclaims 'How pleasant'. Also, certain unnecessary words have disappeared. Both Aunt Mavis and Caleb are suspicious when they hear Dominick bring back the words 'actually' and 'of course'.

And so Dominick sneaks away from his steady and ordered world for a peep at our confused times. He is fascinated and exhilarated. He has much he could tell us, (about smoking, for example!), but at the same time he is an innocent in what seems to him a foreign land. Jane is irresistibly exciting to him. And Dominick is delightfully different from anyone she has ever known. But if he were to take her back, she would suffer the fate of the rose.

Jeremy Paul, June 1987

The Cast

Dominick Hide
Alaric Maze
Caleb Line
Ava
Jane Winters
Jim Bone
Felix
Midge
Harry Shoe
Brian
Great Aunt Mavis
Helda (Dominick's mother)
Geoffrey
Carole
Three youths (Battersea pub)
Policeman
Traveller (on Bullet)
Old market lady
Dominick Schwartz
Barman
Gordon (pools)
Rose-seller (pub)
Angry woman
Anxious mother
Ida
Haruld
Carl Morgan
Young Jonathan
Waiter (bistro)
Guitarist (bistro)
Lorry driver

Holograms

Musical trio
Lute-player
Spanish dancer
Voices of Magi and Soo female computers

The Flip Side of Dominick Hide

1 An aerial view of London

It is 1980 and traffic is pouring over Westminster Bridge, and boats pushing their way up river.

Suddenly the image magnifies, with a closer view of a red London Transport bus crossing the bridge. A 'view-finder' frame has appeared, surrounding the picture.

It follows the bus in close-up along the South Bank until it is obscured by a building.

The scene is now a wide-angle view of London from about one thousand feet up. The picture tilts slightly, the setting sun being followed by clouds and blue sky. We are in an ultra-modern craft and climbing fast.

The view outside is no longer blue but the blackness of space, and the curvature of the earth stretches across one corner of the windscreen.

A vast flying-saucer landing 'field'. An immense cartwheel-shaped complex with pods at the end of each 'spoke'. A saucer with winking lights is seen locking into one of the pods.

2 Inside the Saucer

Dominick Hide is guiding his craft in. He is in his late twenties, good-humoured, an expert at his job – but at this moment he seems preoccupied and disappointed.

He runs his fingers over a series of sensor buttons on his left panel which glow to his touch. At his right he punches two projected discs. As Dominick's flying saucer materialises, it glides slowly towards its landing pod.

The lights are dimming now and Dominick's saucer is the last to lock in, his lights winking and blinking on their own.

He talks his way through the routine landing procedure with Alaric Maze, his partner-mechanic.

DOMINICK Blocks secure?
ALARIC (*his voice distorted*) Yet. Two. (*bleep bleep*)
DOMINICK (*touching a sensor*) Rollers pinned?
ALARIC Yet. Four. (*four bleeps*)
DOMINICK Hauser locked?
ALARIC Yet. One zero. (*bleep*)
DOMINICK Exit cleared?

The last four bleeps are the last four notes of the National Anthem. The hum of the engine dies down. Dominick has been releasing five long thin laser tubes and packing them into a briefcase.

ALARIC You're two minutes late.
DOMINICK (*with a wry smile*) Yes. I had to wait for a bus.

He picks up his lunchbox, a snap-tight see-through container, and opens the top of the saucer.
As he walks along the corridor streams of pink lights crisscross him: he is undergoing the decontamination routine.
He stops at the mirror face-scan and grimaces comically. The door opens before him and the pink crisscross lights go out, as he comes through into the reception area.
Alaric is checking a small instrument panel and blowing his nose. He is a fat, jovial man in his thirties.

ALARIC (*agitated*) You were right on failsafe today, what were you doing?
DOMINICK (*smiling*) Bouncing on the limits – to see if you were awake.

He removes the laser tubes from his case, hands them over to Alaric and starts getting out of his flight suit.

ALARIC You know the dorn limits! Two hundred metres. You almost stopped my heart. (*he sneezes*)
DOMINICK You should take a cure for that.

Magi, the female computer speaks.

MAGI Coro 42 report to Mr Line, please.
DOMINICK (*surprised*) Why, Magi?
MAGI Coro 42 report to Mr Line. No reason given . . . Dominick.
ALARIC He's following my read-out. (*he examines the tube*) You've only documented three and a half tubes . . .
DOMINICK (*with sudden irritation*) Traffic jam!

Alaric stares at his friend, puzzled.

3 Caleb Line's Office

Caleb lives in his office, a small comfortable room. A benign, eccentric man in his sixties, he is pouring tea from a futuristic samovar.

CALEB Tea, Dominick?
DOMINICK No thank you, Caleb.
CALEB Few people do these days. I hate to see the old customs die out. Sit down. Complacent with your mission, Dominick?

Dominick nods politely.

CALEB Amusing, the history of Transport ... we've made a modicum of progress? We can regulate our trips to microseconds. Take punctuality for granted.
DOMINICK Yes.
CALEB So why were you two minutes late on your double-return? Machine fault?
DOMINICK No, I'm sorry ...
CALEB I accept apology. Reason?
DOMINICK (*calmly*) It was raining. Rain slows everything. I saw an old woman knocked down. I was checking how long before help reached her. The medicar was blocked in progress. I think she died.
CALEB So?
DOMINICK I thought it might be interesting.
CALEB (*after a pause*) People are not your conspectus, Dominick. If you wish to study people, watch old films.

Dominick is surprised by the sudden coldness of his tone.

4 The Underground Bullet-Train

Dominick's fellow travellers are placid, at ease – they show no sign of rush hour strain.
But he looks strained. He is wrestling with a problem – his growing desire to land his craft on the flip side (1980).
After a moment he raises his hand to his mouth, and quietly whistles the first four notes of Ba-Ba Black Sheep into a ring on his finger.

DOMINICK Soo – is Ava home?

(*Soo is the household computer.*)

SOO   Ava returned seven minutes ago, Dominick. She is taking a shower.
DOMINICK   (*surprised*) Is is working again?
SOO   (*distorted*) The jet was repaired this morning, Dominick. At your request.
DOMINICK   Good. Tell Ava I'm twelve minutes late, Soo. Nothing strange.

Whistles last four notes of 'Black Sheep' and lowers his hand. A man beside him is working out a computerized crossword.

MAN   Several people go off the deep end. Six letters.
DOMINICK   (*promptly*) Divers.

The man nods his thanks, and clicks the letters into place. Behind Dominick we see the dial of underground stops:
Rotherhythe – Tower – Picadilly – Bush – Alperton – Rayners Lane. This confirms the feeling we already have: that we are still in London, at some future date.
We see the light move from Picadilly to Bush – as the train glides smoothly, silently on its way – and during this we catch snippets of other nursery tunes (the current fad) being whistled, as commuters reports their progress home.

5 Dominick's Home. Night

A living room, kitchen area, and a bedroom with shower cabinet. Ava sits watching a hologram of a musical trio in Mediaevil Costume playing The Beatles song Yesterday. Dominick comes in. Their life together is pleasant, uncomplicated. They were found for each other by computer and are therefore completely compatible.

AVA   (*with a brief glance*) Hey Dominick.
DOMINICK   Hey Ava.

He touches her shoulder lightly by way of greeting, then walks through the hologram and makes for the bedroom, and shower.

AVA   Easy day?
DOMINICK   Like all. A waste of time! I think I'm being censured.
AVA   What have you done?

She comes to the door with slight concern. He is undressing for a shower.

DOMINICK (*with a resigned shrug*) Nothing. Watch people in lines wait for buses which come three together, fill up and travel past more people in lines ... in the rain ... wait for buses which have not left the terminal.

She goes to pour him a drink.

DOMINICK Who is amused by this? And why am *I* sent to record it?
AVA It's interesting. It measures our progress.
DOMINICK Your work in interesting. With ThomCook ... you have variation with sightsee tours. Where did *you* go today?
AVA (*hands him a drink*) Olympics, 1936. Strange happening ... a traveller started banging his head at the window and cried 'let me out' ...
DOMINICK (*puzzled smile*) Why? Did he want to compete?
AVA He was ninety seven. We had to put him to sleep. Why did he feel an urge to join orderless times?
DOMINICK (*thoughtfully*) Perhaps he had something to go back for. Something he wanted to do.

He turns on the shower.

AVA (*slight laugh*) The tours are arranged to comfort us, you know, to make us complacent. Have you ever seen war on the flip side ... Dominick?

But he hasn't heard. Busy in the shower, he turns the shower from water to drying, and grins at her in triumph.

DOMINICK Jet's working!
AVA Yes. (*she smiles*) Ready to eat?

He nods.

AVA Your mother scanned. Has news for you.

Dominick steps out of the shower.
Ava goes into the kitchen sector. She takes a large pill from a container, and puts it into a high-speed micro-wave oven.
Dominick appears, informally dressed, sips his drink and bleeps his mother onto a screen.

DOMINICK Hey Mother.
HELDA (*an elegant lady of 50*) Dominick dear. I have the right person to answer your question.
Beside me.

INTENSIVE CARE

A spry old lady appears on the screen, great Aunt Mavis, 115 years old.

HELDA   Aunt Mavis.

MAVIS   Dominick, you naughty boy, you never visit me.

DOMINICK   (*sheepish*) Aunt Mavis I promise I'll come and play Scrabble with you, soon as I end my mission. What have you found me?

Ava turns to listen with interest.

MAVIS   Your great-great grandfather ... my grandfather whom I never knew ... *was* living in London, 1980. In a sector called Port ... Beale, I think. You are named after him, Dominick.

DOMINICK   (*eagerly*) What else do you know? What age was he? How did he fill his days?

MAVIS   Don't be impatient, I'm doing my best, I'm searching for a roll of cine. Of him as a boy. It's documented but I can't find it. Our family records are in shaming disorder.

HELDA   Why are you curious, Dominick?

DOMINICK   (*offhand*) It's our family history, Mother. Nothing strange. Thank you, Aunt Mavis. You'll keep looking?

MAVIS   What, dear?

DOMINICK   You will look for that film?

MAVIS   Don't shout. Speak carefully.

HELDA   Don't tire Mavis, Dominick.

MAVIS   I'm *not* tired, Helda.

DOMINICK   Thank you, Aunt Mavis. Goodbye, Mother.

Dominick fades them both out, sits back.
Ava brings supper which is now transformed into two plates of roast beef, Yorkshire pudding, veg, etc.
Dominick summons Soo.

DOMINICK   Soo ... London, 1980. Port Beale. Locate, please.

SOO   (*a disembodied voice*) Yes, Dominick.

AVA   (*puzzled*) You shouldn't be over London if you have a relative on the circuit. It's forbidden. There must be a computerror, Dominick. You should tell Caleb.

DOMINICK   Yes ... I should. (*he starts eating*)

SOO   There is no sector in London, 1980 – Port Beale, Dominick.

DOMINICK   Are you sure? Check again.

SOO There is no sector in London, 1980 – Port Beale. Double check.

6 Dominick's House, Next Day

Alaric is playing pool with his lady partner, Ida, a skinny girl with crooked teeth and a happy disposition.
The table is black with silver balls which disappear in lieu of being pocketed.
Alaric plays an unsuccessful shot. Ava takes over and is also unsuccessful.
Dominick is pouring wine.

ALARIC (*crosses to Dominick*) Your shoot, Ida.
DOMINICK (*urgently*) Alaric . . . .
ALARIC Claims she was school champ in her programme. But I take *that* with a pinch of salt.
DOMINICK (*quietly*) Alaric . . .
ALARIC (*surprised*) Good pot. On Ida!
DOMINICK I want to land. Monday.
ALARIC What? No sense.
DOMINICK I want to land and you'll help me, friend. One hour. All I need. You can deflect from Caleb. You know you can.
ALARIC (*whispers*) I'm complacent! I like my job. Why do I risk it because you're zooloonie!

Taps his head, meaning 'nuts'.

DOMINICK I know he's on the flip side. On my circuit. I must meet him. Once. No danger. You shield me.
ALARIC Landing is forbidden for good reasons. Remember Teddy Cochrane.
AVA Who's Teddy Cochrane?
DOMINICK I was telling Alaric about your Olympic traveller in 1936 – the one you K.O.'d for the journey when he wished to land. Why you couldn't land him, even though he wanted to.

Ava still looks puzzled.
Alaric starts to tell the story, pointedly, for Dominick's benefit, to remind him of the dangers.

ALARIC There was a Coro called Teddy Cochrane, Ava . . . landed in Ohio, US in 1955. Against orders. Killed a dog.

	Changed history. Dog was going to raise alarm for a fire. (*shrugs*) Wasn't there to do it. People died in the blaze who should have lived. One of them an architect ... whose buildings fell down because he wasn't there to build them.!
AVA	What happened to the occupants?
ALARIC	You've heard of the Missing Persons Bureau? People vanished right through the line. Whole families ... and all because of Cochrane and a dog.
IDA	Skuse! (*all the balls have gone*) I've won!
ALARIC	(*amazed*) How pleasant!
AVA	Too good!
IDA	What happened to Cochrane?
ALARIC	When he knew what he'd done, Ida, he went dupe. Died in an asylum six years ago. Another?

He pushes a button and all the balls re-appear.

AVA	You play first, Dominick.

He plays the shot. Alaric watches him with guarded interest.

7 Inside the Saucer

Alaric is making small adjustments to the flight panel.
Dominick, ready for take-off, appears at the top, looking down.

ALARIC	All set, Mr Cochrane. No sweat, Mr Cochrane. Chip chopped and ready to go.
DOMINICK	You're a wizard. Will Magi know?
ALARIC	I've blinded her – and Caleb. Now remember, when you touch ground, switch everything off. Let it cool for forty seconds.

Alaric eases past him out of the craft and hands him a flattened black hat.

ALARIC	Don't forget this.
DOMINICK	What for?
ALARIC	Pollute protection. It might be raining. Chosen your landing site?
DOMINICK	(*getting down into his seat*) Yes, I've marked one.
ALARIC	Might look different in the dark.
DOMINICK	No danger. Ease down.
ALARIC	Bring back one of the women. I think I'm out of step with the modern female. (*he goes*)

The lid closes, the engine starts humming. Lights start flashing.

ALARIC (*anxiously*) No mistakes Dominick.

DOMINICK I'll watch out for dogs.

Dominick looks out into blackness – then sees the outer rim of the earth reappearing in the corner, and then sees it enlarging. Getting closer, he sees a whirl of lights on black, slowly focussing into the city at night.

Dominick works the controls with concentrated precision, as the ground rises up at him. As mysterious as the face of the moon: it's a wasteland in Battersea. The craft materializes, hovers, then hits the ground with a gentle bump.

He sits for a moment, adjusting to the pressure, and the enormity of his action. He switches off all panels.

8 On the Wasteland. Outside

The saucer sits there like a dead hunk of metal, totally silent for forty seconds. Then slowly the lid opens and Dominick's head appears. On it sits the hat, also saucer-shaped – like a Catholic priest's hat.

Dominick peers into the blackness, adjusting to the new wonderland, and the night sounds of London, faint at first then building to exaggerated intensity. He puts his hand to his head, until these settle to their normal level.

His wonderland is in fact a derelict piece of ground, seemingly deserted apart from a few trees and some abandoned cars. He steps out carefully. A dog barking nearby stops him in his tracks. Silence. He is about to start walking again when he hears noises and giggling nearby.

GEOFFREY What you wearin' under this, thermal bloomers?

Carole laughs in protest.

Dominick steps near to investigate and sees couple in a passionate clinch behind a bush.

GEOFFREY You are about to experience a delight not of this world Carole . . .

CAROLE (*screams*) Geoffrey!

GEOFFREY (*flustered*) What is it? What's the matter?

He rolls over and looks in the direction she is pointing. Dominick stands near them with his hat raised and a polite smile. For him sex is not a particularly surprising or private thing.

DOMINICK   Skuse ...
GEOFFREY   What do you want?
CAROLE   It's a vicar!
DOMINICK   Can you tell me the way to Port Beale?
GEOFFREY   Pork veal? You want a butcher's, mate.
DOMINICK   (*puzzled*) Butchers?
GEOFFREY   Look, go and ask in that pub over there. Can't you see we're engaged ... busy!
DOMINICK   Thank you. Good night.

He makes his way to a fence, finds a hole in it and disappears through it.

GEOFFREY   That weren't no vicar. That was a peepin' Tom. (*turns back to Carole*)
CAROLE   My God, Geoffrey, look, he's praying!
GEOFFREY   Don't look. (*He takes her back into his arms.*)

9 A London Street

Dominick crawls through the fence and finds himself staring slowly up at a Police Constable on the beat.

OFFICER   Been to a party, have we, sir? (*Then he eyes Dominick's hat*) Or was it bell-ringing tonight?

Dominick is totally confused by this.

OFFICER   If you're thinkin' of grabbin' one for the road (*indicating the pub*) I'm afraid you're unlucky, they've just closed, so I'd go quietly home if I was you. Far to go, have you?

Dominick shakes his head.

OFFICER   I take it you are travellin' on shanks' pony.
DOMINICK   (*bewildered*) Yes.
OFFICER   (*nods*) Goodnight, then.

Dominick walks quickly away, across the road to the pub. He sees three young men getting into a van. He takes a deep breath, looks cautiously at the road, then boldly crosses to join them. As he approaches he raises his hat.

DOMINICK   Skuse ... I wish to go to Port Beale.

The three youths are all drunk and cheerful.

YOUTH 1   Not on our route, mate. Sorry.
YOUTH 2   Port where?
DOMINICK   I wish to know the way . . .
YOUTH 3   Don't we all, Bishop! (*climbs in*)
YOUTH 2   Beale . . . Beale . . . Deal . . . in London, is it? (*Dominick nods*)
YOUTH 1   This is Battersea, mate. Port . . . Portsmouth does he mean?
YOUTH 2   Port Talbot?
YOUTH 3   Hang on a minute. Chuck us the A to Z.

He reaches into the van, while the third youth gropes for the A to Z.

YOUTH 1   (*impatiently*) Ain't got all night, Tosh. I got to do me laundry.
YOUTH 2   Hang on . . . good Samaritan, this is.
YOUTH 3   Good Samaritan? That's pub down in Peckham, inn'it?

First youth starts singing 'Take me back to the Black Hills of Dakota'.

YOUTH 2   Now then . . . Port . . . Portobello . . . do you mean the Portobello Road?
DOMINICK   No Port Beale?
YOUTH 2   No, no, no . . . Port-o-bello, thas what you want.
DOMINICK   How far is Portobello?
YOUTH 3   Not round here, padre. You're right off the mark here.
YOUTH 1   (*singing*) . . . to the beautiful Indian Country that I know and love so well!
DOMINICK   Could I take a bus?
YOUTH 2   Not this time of night you couldn't. Ain't you got a bike or somethin'?
YOUTH 1   Come on, give him the ruddy book and get in!
YOUTH 2   (*handing him the book*) Here it is. OneD fifty-nine Weleven one to two hundred and seventy-five and two to two hundred and sixty-two Wten Rem.
DOMINICK   Skuse?
YOUTH 2   (*as the van roars away*) Present. Good luck! (*laughter*)

Dominick stares blankly at the book. Then he moves to a street lamp to study it further.
A dog comes up, growls, sniffs at Dominick who backs away, remembering Cochrane.

INTENSIVE CARE

DOMINICK Go away! Go! Scat!

The dog lingers, then pees against the lampost.
Dominick is horrified at the criminal lack of sanitation of the deed.

DOMINICK Don't *do* that! Bad! Scat! Bad!

The dog, feeling threatened, starts barking, then gives chase as Dominick takes flight, scrambling back through the fence, stuffing the A to Z into his hat, holding tightly onto it.
Pursued by dog snapping at his heels Dominick just makes it to the saucer and disappears back through the lid, slamming it shut behind him.
The dog barks at the saucer, clearly intrigued then stops in surprise as lights flash on and the humming starts.
Geoffrey and Carole are reaching their climax of love-making. Then Carole watches in disbelief as the saucer takes off, flashing lights shimmering away above her into the starlit sky.

CAROLE Oh . . . oh . . . *oh!* (*Geoffrey thinks her delight is thanks to him.*) Oh Geoffrey . . . oh my God . . . lights an' hummin' and bright amazing' lights . . . up in the sky . . .

GEOFFREY (*smiling with satisfaction*) Well, I did warn you, Carole.

Carole passes out.

GEOFFREY (*alarmed*) Carole?

10 Dominick's house. Evening

The hologram of the lute player is playing in the background.
Dominick has just related the events to Alaric. They both have drinks.

ALARIC (*incredulous*) Zookers!

DOMINICK Proof! A man gave me a book. Here. I shall find him in Portobello. Next flip.

He brings out the A to Z. The book, exposed to the air, immediately disintegrates with age.
Dominick stares at the dust in his hands in dismay.

ALARIC (*laughing*) If you bring things back you must keep them snaptight shut for ever. You should know that, Dominick.

Ava enters, back from weightless volleyball.

DOMINICK What if I bring you a woman?
AVA Hey, Alaric. What woman?

Dominick seeing Ava indicates behind her back that Alaric mustn't give the game away.

ALARIC Dominick has promised to land on the flip side, 1980 and bring me back a woman as good as you, Ava. But I think she'll disintegrate with age.
AVA (*smiles*) What happened to Ida?
ALARIC I returned her. Not compat. She drank tea in the morning and painted her toes.
AVA Her *toes*?
ALARIC Red. The nails red.
AVA (*concerned*) The computer must be at fault.
DOMINICK Or incorrectly programmed.
ALARIC I feed it all my needs . . . and it provides me Ida.

He flings his arms up in mock despair.
Dominick touches Ava's shoulder affectionately.

DOMINICK Who won volleyball?
AVA (*proudly*) We did.
ALARIC Is it weightless volleyball?
AVA Oh yes. It's more amusing. Shall we go to bed, Dominick? (*he nods*) I'll make drinks.

She goes to the kitchen area.

ALARIC I'd like to try it . . . (*the volleyball*) but I think I might never come down!

Patting his expansive stomach and staring up at the ceiling.
Dominick takes it as a dig at his own daring to land – which Alaric means it to be.

DOMINICK A goal, my friend . . . that's all you need. Goodnight.

Ava brings two steaming mugs from the kitchen.
Dominick puts his arm on her shoulder and leads her into the bedroom.

AVA Goodnight, Alaric.
ALARIC Night.
DOMINICK (*turning back, whispering*) Tomorrow I find Portobello.

He follows Ava into the bedroom.
Alaric sits for a moment, musing, then finishes his drink.
Sound of the shower next door.

ALARIC Goodnight, Soo.

He puts down his glass, and walks through the lute-player towards the main door.

SOO Goodnight, Alaric. Safe home.

He goes out.
Soo automatically fades out the lute-player, and then dims the lights.

11 Dominick's Bedroom. Night

In bed, Dominick rolls gently away from Ava, after making formal love to her.

DOMINICK Thank you, Ava.
AVA Thank you, Dominick. Goodnight.

She closes her eyes. He remains awake, thinking of the morning.

12 A Fairground. Dawn

Nothing is stirring.
A flying saucer sits unnoticed among the entertainments.
Dominick is standing in Portobella Market, as Saturday morning market activity bustles around him. Faces, stalls, shops – and also a dog which makes him momentarily nervous.
Then he sees Jim Bone, a tall thin young man, wheeling some dresses on a rail down the street past him.
Jim Bone is about twenty-eight, a shambling, lazy, humorous man.

DOMINICK Skuse?

Jim stops, not surprised to see a man dressed strangely in a priest's hat.

DOMINICK I'm looking for Mr Hide. Dominick Hide.
JIM Dominick Hide ... Dominick ... Dominick ... (*then unexpectedly shouting*) Anyone know Dominick Hide?

Dominick starts a little at the volume of Jim's bellow. Various people shake their heads.

VOICE (*from a vegetable stall*) Who wants him?
DOMINICK He's a relative of mine.
JIM (*inventing freely*) His long-lost cousin wants him. Just back from a spell up the Amazon giving Christianity to the Wam-Wams.

Dominick looks puzzled.

JIM Where are you from actually?
DOMINICK Rayner's Lane . . . (*cautiously minicking that word*) actually.
JIM (*after a moment's surprise.*) Yes, of course. Well I'm going the whole length of the road, if he's here should bump into him. Follow me.
DOMINICK (*again mimicking a new word*) Of course.

Fascinated, he falls into step behind Jim and the dresses. He sees Jim talking to an old market woman and hears:

OLD WOMAN Dominick? He wants Dominick? He's over there where he always is of a Saturday.

She points.
Jim returns with the information and points to a stall with hand-painted sign Dominic.

JIM Mission accomplished. He's over there. Ta-ta.

He wheels on with the dresses.
With mounting excitement Dominick approaches the stall.

DOMINICK (*tentatively*) Er . . . Dominick?

A smiling West Indian stall-holder turns and looks enquiringly at him.
Dominick smiles, tips his hat, passes on through crowd, and catches Jim up as he is about to enter a junk shop.

DOMINICK Wrong man.
JIM Oh well . . . mmh . . . let's ask the lady in here.

13 Jane's Shop

It seems empty – then laughter is heard from the back.

JIM Jane?

Jane emerges – she's an attractive carelessly dressed girl in her late twenties.

JANE She's had kittens in the night! Four! Merle's had four kittens.
JIM By which husband?
JANE Otto is my guess. He's out on the roof looking pleased with himself.

She starts to inspect the dresses.

Are these from Swindon?

JIM Yeh – he couldn't get his lorry down the road, so I took 'em off him and wheeled 'em down. Here's your receipt.

He hands her the receipt and goes to inspect the kittens, leaving Dominick forgotten.
Dominick stares at Jane, immediately intrigued by her.
She smiles at him, assuming he's a customer.

JANE Can I help?
DOMINICK No I'm . . . looking . . .
JANE O.K. Feel free.
DOMINICK I'm looking for a man named Dominick Hide.
JIM (*from the back*) Got names for them yet?
JANE (*calling back*) Don't even know what sex they are yet. (*to Dominick*) There's no-one here called Dominick. Sorry.

She joins Jim with the kittens.
Dominick stands undecided.

JANE (*whispers to Jim*) Who's your friend?
JIM Mmh? He still here?

They see Dominick examining an African spear.

He's looking for his cousin.

JANE What's he wearing?
JIM I think he belongs to some sort of religious order, at an educated guess. The hat's religious.

Jane shrugs, decides to come back and investigate Dominick further.
He has moved on to some antique objects.

JANE That's from Mesopotamia.

Dominick puts down the mask.

Exact date unknown. I'm sorry to be nosey but could I just feel the material of your suit.

He allows her to touch his sleeve.

What is it?

DOMINICK I don't know. I bought it in . . . Dakota. (*He says this out of panic*) Goodbye, I must continue my search.
JANE Can we help? What does your cousin do?
DOMINICK I haven't seen him for many years. I heard he was in Portobello.
JIM Is he a boozer?
DOMINICK (*cautiously*) He might be.
JIM Let's go and find out. Jane?
JANE Got to sort these out. Join you in a minute.

Jim strides out.
Dominick hesitates, and gives Jane a look, which she returns.
Then he follows Jim.

14 A Pub

Jim brings two pints from the bar towards Dominick who sits alone, adjusting to the new atmosphere.
Felix and Midge enter. Felix is bearded, opinionated, mid-thirties. Midge is small, freckly, Irish, in her twenties: Felix's long-suffering girl.

FELIX Thank you, James. We'll have the same.
JIM Get it yourself. (*they do*)

Jim places the pints in front of Dominick who eyes them cautiously.

DOMINICK What is this?
JIM This? It's real ale. Don't you drink beer?
DOMINICK I drink wine actually. Of course. (*drinks*) It's good.
JIM You've been living abroad, have you? Just back in England? (*Dominick nods, as Jim drinks.*) Funny that. You said you lived in Rayners Lane.

Dominick is saved by Midge and Felix approaching with pints.

MIDGE Hi.
DOMINICK Hey . . .
JIM Midge. Felix. This is . . .
DOMINICK Hide.
FELIX (*jumpy*) Where?
DOMINICK Skuse?

JIM   Hide, of course. But what's your first name?

For a moment Dominick is stuck – then he sees a name on a bottle of gin behind the bar.

DOMINICK   Gilbey.
MIDGE   Hi Gilbey.
JIM   (*shaking his hand*) Jim Bone.
FELIX   (*gloomily*) We've just been evicted.
JIM   Again?
MIDGE   We owe six weeks rent and Felix threw a punch at the landlord. So we're on the run as well.
DOMINICK   On the . . . runs?
MIDGE   The Law's after us.
FELIX   It's hopeless. Can't go on. It's all falling apart. I give it five years.
DOMINICK   Give what?
FELIX   The whole system . . . the economy . . . Western life. Fiasco.
MIDGE   Felix is an economist. He's writing a book advocating a new monetary system which gets rid of money altogether. Trouble is he can't get past chapter two.
DOMINICK   Why not?
MIDGE   He can't afford the paper.

Dominick smiles at this vision of despair around him.

FELIX   It's not funny!
JIM   (*offering cigarettes*) How do you see the future, Gilbey?
DOMINICK   Me? Well . . . you're not using those, are you? They destroy your body!

They stare at him, poised to light up.

They do!
JANE   (*coming back*) Any luck?
JIM   Oh, we haven't been looking. Is he here, Gibley?
MIDGE   Who?
JANE   (*smiles at the name*) Gilbey . . . That's unusual.
JIM   (*to Midge*) We're looking for Gilbey's long lost cousin Dominick. He's come all the way from Rayners Lane . . .
JANE   Via Dakota where he bought his suit . . .
JIM   To find him.

THE FLIP SIDE OF DOMINICK HIDE

Dominick smiles uneasily, aware he's being teased.

JANE Whose round it is?
DOMINICK I'll get you a drink. Real Ale?
JANE Just a half, thank you, Gilbey.

She sits. They get on with their cigarettes, as Dominick makes for the bar.

DOMINICK A half real ale, please.
BARMAN Half a pint, you mean?
DOMINICK No. Real Ale.
BARMAN Yeh.

Dominick watches him pour the drink and hand it to him.

DOMINICK Thank you.

Dominick goes without paying: the barman whistles: he turns back.

BARMAN It's not a Free House, you know.
DOMINICK Skuse?
BARMAN (*sarky*) Excuse me. Twenty five p.
DOMINICK (*smiles*) Yes. (*starts away*)
BARMAN No. Twenty five p. Money. Comprenez?
DOMINICK Oh money. Twenty five peas?
BARMAN That's right.
DOMINICK (*worried*) I have no . . . peas.
BARMAN (*takes the drink back*) Well I'll guard this, while you try and raise it.

Dominick nods, goes.

I blame the Common Market myself. (*to another customer*)

Dominick goes back to the table.
Felix lifts his near-empty glass.

FELIX Oh mine's a pint, thank you Gilbey.
DOMINICK Like Felix. No peas. Excuse me.
JANE (*amused*) I'll get it.

She goes for her drink. Dominick stands awkwardly. A gypsy rose-seller is selling single red roses nearby.

MIDGE How did you get here from Rayners Lane without any money, Gilbey?
DOMINICK Oh I walked.

Jane returns with her drink, while the others consider Dominick's answer.

MIDGE What do you do for a living?
DOMINICK Travel.
FELIX And sell things or what?
DOMINICK (*trying to joke*) I sell my hat.

Midge takes it from him, puts it on, and preens. Jim takes it from her and examines it.

JIM Yes I should think there's quite a call for these in Rayners Lane.
DOMINICK It protects your face from u.v. rays.
JIM Hear that, Jane, it protects your head from u.v. rays.

He plops it on her head.
The rose-seller is at the table. Dominick stares at the roses with fascination.

FELIX Shove off.
DOMINICK I want a rose.
JANE (*intrigued at his interest*) OK I'll buy you one.

She buys one and presents it to Dominick, and watches him smell it with almost reverential wonder.

SELLER God bless you, darlin'. (*she moves on*)
DOMINICK Thank you.

He sees them watching him curiously.

We don't have these in Rayners Lane.

Then Dominick sees the pub clock: ten past twelve.

DOMINICK I have to go!
JIM Where?
DOMINICK Hat please. I must go.

Jane hands him back his hat.

JANE What about your cousin?
DOMINICK Another day. Thank you for real ale and the rose. Goodbye.

Amazed, they watch him rush out.

FELIX Nutter!
JIM The gear is definitely religious. I'd say he belongs to an

obscure order living the simple life in a suburban house in Rayners Lane.

MIDGE (*giggling*) Celibate?

JIM Well self sufficient certainly. They brew their own wine. And he's been sent out to reclaim a runaway brother. Which accounts for his pig-ignorance of all the important things in life. (*he drinks his ale*)

JANE Who was the rose for?

Running back to the saucer, Dominick sees Harry Shoe, the middle-aged fairground owner inspecting it. He has already roped it off. A small black boy aged ten is also watching with mild curiosity.

HARRY This yours?
DOMINICK Yes.
HARRY Barny sent you with it, did he?
DOMINICK Barny?
HARRY Barny Simpson from Hemel Hempstead.
DOMINICK Yes. Of course.
HARRY He promised a lucky dip, a Hall of Mirrors, and a couple of dodgems, and you turn up with this. Doesn't even bloody work. How do you get into it?
DOMINICK Through the lid.
HARRY Would you mind showing me?

Dominick gets in, mysteriously opening the lid.

HARRY (*sarky*) Incredible. Can you get the lights working?
DOMINICK I certainly hope so.

He disappears into the saucer.

HARRY If you can get the lights going, tell Barny I'll have it. O.K? (*the lights start flashing*) Fantastic.
DOMINICK (*re-appearing*) I want peas.
HARRY Eh? Garden or frozen? Or do you mean a leak?
DOMINICK Excuse me?
BOY He wants money for it.
HARRY Shut up. All right, how much? (*Dominick looks unsure*) Look here's fifteen quid on account. More than it's worth.

He clambers up to hand over three fivers.

DOMINICK Careful!
HARRY Why, it's not goin' to take off, is it? (*he jumps off*) Stay here a minute. Don't go away.

Dominick watches Harry depart to his office to make a phone call. The boy sees the rose which Dominick is still clutching.

BOY I want that rose. For my mum.
DOMINICK You can't. Stand back. Tell the man I'll be back again soon.
BOY Where yer goin'?
DOMINICK Rayners Lane.

He lowers himself back into the saucer.

15 In the Saucer. Day

Dominick stares at the fivers, unsure how to preserve them. He takes out his lunchbox container, removes cheese from a bag, eats the cheese, puts the fivers into the bag, puts the bag into a glove compartment.
Then he lays the rose gently in the lunchbox, snapping the lid shut.

16 Harry's Office

Harry is on the phone to Barny.
A signwriter is already at work on a large board – 'Genuine Flying Saucer – the only one in captivity'.

HARRY (*on phone*) All right Barny, forget the dodgems, forget everything you owe me, I'll give it a two week trial, and if it pays we'll call it quits, now I can't say fairer than that, can I? What?

Barny's reply is garbled – he doesn't know what Harry is on about but he's shrewd enough to know he's on to a good thing.

HARRY Look I've already given your man fifteen! Well how much percentage? ... you're joking, look I'll give you two and a half on the first week and we'll see how we go from there ... that's my final offer, Barny. (*slams down the phone*) Bloody crook!

17 The Fairground

The boy solemnly watches the saucer take off, with lights flashing – and spin away into thin air.
Harry comes from his office, just missing this. He joins the boy and

stares bemused at the scorched earth marks where the saucer recently stood.

HARRY Where the hell's he gone?
BOY He took off.
HARRY Don't be bloody smart with me, Jonathan.

He starts searching behind the merry-go-round.

BOY (*calling after him*) Said he'd be back again soon.

18 Dominick's House. Night

Ava stares at the rose in the container. She is about to open the lid.

DOMINICK Don't! It'll vaporize. (*takes it from her*) It must stay just as it is.

Puts it on the table.

AVA What have you done, Dominick?
DOMINICK Sit down. (*she obeys*) The rose is a present – from the flip side. It's a hundred and fifty years old. And it smells like no rose we've ever known.
AVA (*faintly*) You landed?
DOMINICK Twice. It's safe. Alaric controls it. Caleb knows nothing.
AVA You break the rules.
DOMINICK No censure, please. You remember your Olympic traveller who banged on the window? I have to find someone. I have friends to help me.
AVA Friends . . . on the flip side? Do they know where you're from?
DOMINICK (*smiles*) Yes. Rayners Lane. Nothing strange. I'm brighter than they.
AVA If all coros landed . . .
DOMINICK They won't. You say nothing. I trust you, Ava.
AVA You trouble me. I'm not prepared. What are these words we're saying? I don't know you, Dominick.
DOMINICK I'm not different. I'm seeking knowledge. Support me. Share it. I need you with me.
AVA I can't come with you!
DOMINICK No you mistake. I ask you to travel with me . . . in your heart.
AVA But danger . . . Cochrane . . . the dog . . .
DOMINICK (*gently*) Ease down. I watch where I go.

AVA Caleb watches everything. Dominick . . . you'll spoil our style. It's not our function to find knowledge. We're not trained for it.

She looks at him, puzzled rather than disturbed.

DOMINICK If you wish to be re-programmed . . .
AVA No. In other things, I'm content with you. (*pause*) I'll serve supper.

19 Jane's Shop

Jane is laughing at Dominick who stands before her – without his hat.

JANE You've sold your hat!
DOMINICK Not needed, I think.
JANE I thought you looked rather nice in it.

They look at each other for a moment.

DOMINICK Have you found my cousin?
JANE Oh . . . were you expecting us to?
DOMINICK It's why I'm here.
JANE (*lightly*) Thought you'd come to see me.
DOMINICK Yes, of course. And Jim and Felix and Midge and the woman who sells roses. And the kittens.
JANE We lost one of them. (*she opens the phonebook*) What was the name, Hide? H.I.D.E. – as in hide and seek?

Dominick nods, puzzled.

JANE Hide, D.A. the only one. Lives in Maida Vale. Not far away. Ring him. (*hands him the phone book, pointing to the number*) Go on.
DOMINICK (*hesitates*) Will you . . .?

Jane shrugs, picks up the phone and starts dialling.

JANE Does he owe you money?
DOMINICK Money? No, my Great Aunt Mavis sent me. She wants me to find her lost grandson. She lives in Hemel Hempstead.
JANE Hello . . . Mr Dominick Hide?

Dominick holds his breath.

JANE I see. Thank you. Sorry to trouble. (*she puts the phone down*) That was Donald Hide. No Dominick.

Dominick is disappointed, but also a bit relieved.

JANE Look I'm closing up and I've got to get all this across to my flat. (*pointing to a pile of clothes*) You couldn't give me a hand, could you? It's just round the corner.

20 Jane's Flat. Evening

A large bed-sitter with kitchen and bathroom off it, and full of unusual clutter. Jane leads the way in – Dominick is piled up with clothes.

JANE Dump 'em anywhere.

He does.

JANE I must have a bath, I've been rummaging around a warehouse all day. Filthy. Make yourself some coffee if you like. Through there. (*indicating the kitchen*) I'll have some too.

She goes into the bathroom, starts running the bath.
Dominick stares in amazement at the room, so unlike his own, but oddly comforting. He checks a small clock by the bed then, reassured, he goes into the kitchen area.
He finds a jar marked coffee, opens it, sniffs it – it is unfamiliar. He looks round, finds two mugs, takes a tablespoon and scoops out coffee into the mugs. It doesn't seem enough, so he adds more. Then stops – he doesn't know what to do next. The phone goes. Jane comes to answer it, in a dressing gown. He watches her light a cigarette.

JANE I'll get it. Hello, Jim. No not tonight I'm knackered . . . no I can't be persuaded . . . yes, quite alone unless you count a celibate priest. No you can't come over. Mind your own business. (*rings off*)

DOMINICK (*awkwardly, into the room*) I'm . . . unable . . .

JANE Oh don't say the kettle's bust again.

She comes past him, checks the kettle for water and finding it already full she forces the plug in and switches on.

JANE You just have to jam it in. See? It's working. I won't be long. Make yourself at home.

Jane goes back to the bathroom.
Dominick surveys the hissing kettle, mystified. He looks round the kitchen, sees a travel calendar, flips ahead a few months and finds a picture of Quito, Equador.
He then becomes alarmed at the noise of the kettle and quickly switches it off, before it has boiled. Gingerly he pours the water into the mugs, making tepid sludge. He stirs it with the tablespoon, tastes it, grimaces.
He shrugs, then picks up the mugs and takes them directly to the bathroom, leaving one on the table on the way.
Jane, now in the bath, is so amazed by his intrusion that she makes only a token effort to cover up. Dominick shows no surprise at the naked female form – prudery is not an issue of his time.
He hands her the coffee: she takes it with an incredulous laugh.

JANE Thank you, Gilbey, I'll be out in a minute.

But he's seen her toes.

DOMINICK You paint your toes?
JANE Yes. Sorry.

She pushes her red toes under the water Dominick is now fascinated by the plumbing.

DOMINICK What are those?
JANE They're taps, aren't they? Where the water comes from? Look I really won't be long if you'd like to wait in the other room.
DOMINICK (*politely*) Of course. If you wish.
JANE Yes I do actually.

He goes nonchalantly, closing the door. She stares, puzzled – then sips the coffee and spits it out, violently. When she emerges, rather flustered but now dressed, Dominick is looking calmly out of the window, his coffee untouched.

JANE You haven't drunk your coffee, Gilbey.
DOMINICK I don't . . . actually . . .
JANE I don't blame you. Let's try some wine, shall we?

She takes the mugs into the kitchen, and finds some wine in the fridge.

JANE You do drink wine?
DOMINICK Yes of course.

She brings back the wine – she is now very intrigued. He seems to be playing games and she decides to clarify a few points.

JANE Well . . . bottoms up, Gilbey.

Dominick's baffled. They both drink. Jane flops into a chair.

JANE OK, what's the game, kiddo?
DOMINICK Volleyball?
JANE (*slightly annoyed*) Oh come on, Gilbey, look I won't tell anyone. What are you up to? Where are you from, and don't say Rayners Lane because I shan't believe you.
DOMINICK What I say – is unbelieving.
JANE Try me.
DOMINICK I come from far away. (*he wants to tell her*)
JANE How far?
DOMINICK (*losing his nerve*) Quitto, Equador.
JANE Quitto? That's how the natives pronounce it?
DOMINICK Lived my life there. (*smiles*) We don't drink coffee.
JANE (*after a pause*) Are you in the Church? Missionary?
DOMINICK I come on a mission.
JANE (*laughs*) To find Dominick Hide for your great aunt Mavis who lives in Hemel Hempstead.
DOMINICK Some of that is true.
JANE Are you married?

He hesitates, unsure of the word.

JANE Sorry. Silly question.
DOMINICK Why?
JANE You don't look married. Are you in some kind of enclosed order where women are forbidden?
DOMINICK Women are not forbidden.
JANE Glad to hear it. Nuns around, are there?
DOMINICK I'm sorry . . . nuns?
JANE Forget it. (*gets up*) Look I'm sorry, I do have rather a lot to do tonight.
DOMINICK We have supper together, OK?

She looks surprised.

DOMINICK I have time for it.
JANE Well I mean . . . there's nothing to eat here. We could go out . . . I suppose. Are you hungry?
DOMINICK (*firmly*) Yes.

21 In a Bistro. Later

Candlelit table, yellow rose in vase, a Spanish guitarist plays moody songs.
Jane is sitting with Dominick over coffee and pudding. She has been drawn into the romantic mood against her better judgement, and is feeling confused.

JANE The shop doesn't make much but it's my own and I enjoy the buying.
DOMINICK Your face is beautiful.
JANE Sorry?
DOMINICK The skin. Beautiful.

He touches it, in a trance. She is touched by the compliment.

JANE I'm afraid I'm not . . . religious, Gilbey.
DOMINICK Religious? Explain.
JANE Well I mean I don't believe in God.
DOMINICK Who does?
JANE Don't you?
DOMINICK Few people left who believe in God. They live deep in woods and sing old forgotten words.
JANE (*laughs*) You are definitely not a priest then.

He shakes his head.

Then what are you, for God's sake! Tell me! What are you hiding, Mr Hide? Gilbey . . . I don't even believe it's your proper name. Nobody's called Gilbey. It's a brand of gin!

The waiter brings the bill.

DOMINICK What do I give?
JANE (*looking at the bill*) You give fourteen pounds ninety six p, including VAT, minus tip. We'll give it together. (*reaches for her bag.*)
DOMINICK No I have the peas . . . quids this time.

Hands over the fifteen pounds.

WAITER Thank you, sir.

Goes off with it, unsure of his tip.

DOMINICK Now I must go.
JANE Where?
DOMINICK Home. Skuse me. (*gets up*)

JANE Don't you want to take me home?
DOMINICK Not permitted.
JANE Who says? Great Aunt Mavis?
DOMINICK Yes. Goodbye.

As the waiter brings four p change.

JANE Gilbey . . . will I see you again?
DOMINICK I hope so.

He goes and walks straight into the guitarist, mistaking him for a hologram. They both crash to the ground.
Jane laughs, then gets her coat and follows Dominick as he scrambles out of the door.

JANE Wait for me!

The waiter comes to the table, sees the four p, and no yellow rose, the guitarist is mouthing oaths, furious.
Outside, Dominick limps towards a lamp-post and leans against it to recover from his fall.

JANE Do you want me to support you to the tube?
DOMINICK No, I find my way.
JANE OK. Goodnight, Gilbey. Thank you for a most unusual evening.

She gives him a friendly peck on the cheek and walks away unhurriedly.
He stands under the lamp-post, stunned by the kiss and its lingering fragrance.

22 In the corridor of the Cartwheel

Dominick, only just on time, hurries to the mirror face-scan, and stops to compose himself.
The door opens to reveal Caleb waiting with Alaric.
Dominick steps through to join them.

CALEB Good evening, Dominick.
DOMINICK Good evening.

He starts the check-in procedure, while Alaric works unobtrusively at the read-out.

CALEB Punctual return. Unlike London Transport of the 1980s.

Dominick smiles, relaxes: Alaric takes the laser tubes, only two of them full – and conceals them from Caleb.
Dominick only just conceals the lunchbox which contains the yellow rose – but not before Alaric has glimpsed it.
Caleb is casually glancing at Alaric's read-out.

CALEB What was interesting in this day's mission?
DOMINICK I found a problem with the Number 15 bus. It has to pass through a market ... at an intersection where a number of people are gathered, buying and selling. The people delay its progress. No surprise it cannot arrive on schedule.

He is about to leave, to shower.

CALEB Hold hard, Dominick. You made your double return at twelve thousand feet. You're visible for several seconds at that level. You know that.

Dominick looks chastened.

I know it's boring to have to zip up so far to cross over, but we must keep saucer sightings to a minimum, do I make myself absolutely clear? Sightings through the ages have all been due to Coros' carelessness at the point of return and double return. I cannot stress the importance of maxim accuracy strongly enough.

DOMINICK Yes, of course, Caleb.
CALEB (*suspicious*) Of course? (*the word is not in common usage*)
DOMINICK Skuse.

Caleb nods, accepting the apology and goes out looking thoughtful. Dominick relaxes again.

CALEB (*coming back*) You're still turning out for me on Sunday?

Dominick looks puzzled.

Cricket! Woking!

Dominick nods. As Caleb goes, Dominick turns to Alaric.

DOMINICK What was he doing here?
ALARIC Routine Vigilance. Nothing strange.

He brings Dominick the lunchbox with the rose out of its hiding place.

	But how much longer, Dominick? You find your ancestor? I'm not doing all this so you can start a rose garden.
DOMINICK	He's there. I know he is. Two more flips.

He takes the rose and goes out.

23 Viewing Theatre. Night

Mavis is running an old period film, from 1980. At first the images are confused.

MAVIS (*irritated*) Who's been interfering with this?

Dominick and his mother, Helda, sit watching.
The images settle – a small boy, barechested, in bathing trunks, plays on a beach. He is building a sandcastle. His T-shirt is lying on the sand, the writing on it is not quite identifiable.

This could be him. Can you tell the year? What's written on his shirt?

She plays the film back, then forward slowly, but the words remain obscure.

Is that Olympics?

DOMINICK	Possible. Nineteen . . . six? Is that a six?
MAVIS	Or eight. Eighty something.
DOMINICK	I imagine him grown up, my age, but he could be a boy. Don't you know what year he was born?
HELDA	Tell me, why do you want this information?
DOMINICK	I'm curious, Mother. Aren't you? That could be your great grandfather.

Helda shrugs – the film moves on: the boy takes the bucket to the water, fills it, brings it back to fill the moat. He grins at the unseen cameraperson happily.

HELDA	What's he doing?
DOMINICK	Building.
HELDA	With sand? No point. The sea takes it.
MAVIS	If that is him, he learnt something. I found a note in father's records. He grew up to be a millionaire. Building swimming pools – and very large jacuzzis. He helped start

INTENSIVE CARE

DOMINICK Can you never remember meeting him?
MAVIS No – but failing memory is one thing we have no cure for, Dominick. He may not have survived the holocaust of 1999.
HELDA (*worried*) You never go back to that, do you, dear?
DOMINICK No, Mother, that circuit's forbidden.

He looks back at the film.

Who was making the cine? Are there notes of that?

The boy is turning to camera, pulling faces.

MAVIS No. Perhaps his father, or a friend? These records were very badly documented.

The film clicks off.

That's all, dear.
DOMINICK Thank you, Aunt Mavis. It was helpful.
HELDA You promise you're not doing anything silly?
DOMINICK No, Mother. I'm not – actually.
MAVIS 'Actually'? I haven't heard that word since I was a child.
HELDA You trouble me, Dominick.

She goes out.
Dominick produces the lunchbox with the yellow rose in it; from under his seat, and presents it to Mavis, as she is clearing away the projector.

DOMINICK For you, Aunt Mavis. It bloomed thirty five years before you were born. Actually. (*he smiles*)
MAVIS Oh Dominick ... you are being naughty.
DOMINICK Yes. You must never open it to try and catch its fragrance. And never tell a living person.

She embraces him with tears in her eyes and whispers.

MAVIS Dominick, I wish I could come with you.

24 Jane's Flat

Dominick arrives to find a party in progress. He is amazed by the noise, the smoke, the music – and the close physical proximity of some of the guests.

JIM   Gilbey! We've stuck an ad in the local paper for Dominick Hide. Told him to contact Jane here. You never know your luck!

He is dragged off by a woman and kissed.
Jane is canoodling with a stranger in the kitchen. She breaks away as she sees Dominick who is wearing his hat.

MIDGE   Look who I've found.

JANE   Gilbey . . . have you got a drink?

She gets him a glass, empties the dregs, wipes it casually and fills it with wine.
Dominick is surprised by the lack of hygiene.

DOMINICK   Thank you.

JANE   It's my birthday! Well don't look so surprised. We all have to have 'em. Where have you been? Was it something I said at the Bistro?

DOMINICK   I've been away.

JANE   You might have sent a postcard.

DOMINICK   A what?

FELIX   We know what you do, Gilbey . . . can't fool us any more.

MIDGE   Oh shut up.

FELIX   You're a Government agent. Spy. That's a spy's hat. You're disguised as a runaway priest.

MIDGE   Oh my God . . .

FELIX   Pretence at innocence . . . it's flannel. What I want to know is which one of us are you tailing?

MIDGE   You can't even stand up . . .

FELIX   (*shaking her off*) Is it me? Or Midge here . . . well known Irish parrot!

MIDGE   Oh you're so boring!

JANE   She's right, Felix, you can be awfully boring.

DOMINICK   Awfully boring.

JANE   Excuse us.

She leads Dominick away into the main room.
They find somewhere to sit, squashed together.

How's Aunt Mavis?

DOMINICK   Perfect health. Your birthday? I have no present . . . no bottle.

JANE   (*above the noise*) Not necessary.

INTENSIVE CARE

DOMINICK Apology . . .
JANE (*leaning towards her*) What? Can't hear you.

Her hair tumbling in his face: her laughter.

DOMINICK You're beautiful . . .

She raises her face to his, smiling.

I remember your kiss on the road. I return it.

He pecks her on the cheek.

JIM Sorry to break this up. Important announcement to make. (*Shouts to room.*) Turn off the music and shut up everyone for a minute. Now we know why we're here, some of us. To celebrate Jane's sixty-fifth birthday.

Cries of shame: Dominick is surprised.

But there's another reason. One of the guests here tonight, Gilbey Hide . . . stand up, Gilbey (*Dominick is pulled to his feet.*) Who's a prelate working for MI5 . . . has also been conducting a search for his long-lost cousin who happens to owe him a fiver. Now through the miracle of the media, and its distinguished mouthpiece, the Kensington Post where an advertisement was placed . . . a man has just walked through the door and declared himself to be the long-lost cousin. Gibley Hide, This is Your Life! All the way from Clapham Common . . . Mr Dominick Hide!

Applause, cheers.
From the sea of faces, a man steps forward – tall about Dominick's age, not unlike him.
He pauses for a moment, then gives Dominick an emotional hug.

MAN Gilbey . . . You've been looking for me?

Dominick nods.

It's good to see you. I must confess I didn't know you existed. My grandmother sent you, did she?

DOMINICK Yes . . .
MAN Haven't seen her for years. Where is she living?
DOMINICK (*stammers*) Hemel Hempstead.

MAN   Really? What's she doing there? The family lost touch. Give me her address, will you, and I'll go and visit her. Is she well? She must be pretty old.

DOMINICK   Very . . . Is it true you're a millionaire?

MAN   Pardon?

DOMINICK   You build swimming pools, don't you, and jacuzzis?

MAN   Who told you that?

DOMINICK   I'm sorry. You may not be doing that – yet.

MAN   As a matter of fact I am in that line of business.

DOMINICK   If you want help on jacuzzis – how to improve them – how to give water its healing powers, I know something about it.

MAN   Healing waters?

DOMINICK   They cure diseases of age. They give longer life and remove discomfort . I have knowledge . . .

MAN   Well, it's very generous of you, Gilbey, I must give serious thought to what you're saying. I'm always interested in new ideas.

The man then bursts into laughter and Jane steps forward purposely.

JANE   Stop it. Look, piss off, will you? Gilbey, I'm sorry, this man isn't your cousin. He's a friend of Jim's who wasn't invited as far as I know.

JIM   Only a joke Gilbey.

DOMINICK   (*shattered*) Joke? What joke?

JANE   (*returning*) Here's your drink.

Dominick takes it, sits down, feeling faint.

MIDGE   My God, he was telling the truth.

FELIX   Wha. . . . .

MIDGE   He really is looking for someone.

25 Dominick's Home. Night

Ava is sitting alone, looking at the red rose with a disturbed expression.

AVA   (*after a moment*) Soo?

SOO   Yes Ava?

AVA   What is Dominick doing now?

SOO He is on a mission. He is studying London Transport, 1980.
AVA Has he landed?
SOO Coros are forbidden to land, Ava.
AVA I know – but has he broken the rules?
SOO (*after a pause*) He cannot break the rules. Coros are forbidden to land on missions.
AVA Then how do you explain this?

She picks up the rose.

Where does it come from? (*Silence*) Did you hear me?

SOO I cannot answer.
AVA Can't or won't?
SOO I cannot answer.
AVA Thank you, Soo.

She stares at the rose, puts the container to her cheek – then slowly starts to open the lid.
For a brief moment she catches the smell. Then the rose begins to wither.
She slams the lid shut – but it continues to die in front of her eyes.
She gives a small gasp.

26 Jane's Flat

The final guests are leaving. Dominick is alone with Jane.

JANE Would you like some coffee?

She starts spraying the room with an aerosol. Dominick grabs the can from her.

DOMINICK Don't do that!
JANE What?
DOMINICK You'll destroy the atmosphere.
JANE I was hoping to improve the atmosphere actually.
DOMINICK Don't use it.

He throws it in the bin.

JANE Didn't know you were into ecology. As well as jacuzzis.
DOMINICK There are some things you must simply obey.

Pause. She smiles.

JANE   Kiss me. (*he hesitates*) There are some things *you* must simply obey. Fair's fair, Gilbey.

He comes to her slowly and kisses her – carefully on the cheek. She turns so that their lips meet for a brief moment. They break, both taken by surprise at the sudden excitement.

JANE   Think I'll just clear some of this . . .
DOMINICK   I have to go . . .
JANE   Now?
DOMINICK   First light.
JANE   There's time yet, I mean . . . It's only half past two . . . we can put the alarm on . . .
DOMINICK   Your lips tasted of . . .
JANE   (*nervous*) Cigarettes?

He kisses her again.

I really must . . . give up . . .

Their kiss becomes more passionate.
Then they break again, slightly breathless.

DOMINICK   Thank you.
JANE   Pleasure . . .
DOMINICK   Again? Without light?

He looks for the light switch.

JANE   It's over there.

Dominick goes to the switch by the door and plunges them into darkness except for a shaft of moonlight.
He crashes into a chair.

Are you all right . . . Gilbey? I'm over here.

He finds her.

DOMINICK   So many things . . .
JANE   I know. Sorry. Shall we sit down? It might be safer.

They sit on the bed, and he takes her in his arms, kissing her and whispering.

DOMINICK   I like you.
JANE   (*responding*) I like you . . .
DOMINICK   So different.
JANE   You too . . .

DOMINICK Do you wish for sex?
JANE Yes . . .
DOMINICK Then I think . . . I think I'll take my shower.
JANE (*breaking away from him*) What?
DOMINICK My custom.
JANE Really? It doesn't work. It's bust. I really don't mind – if you don't. Do you mind if I don't?

He hesitates.

We could have a bath together afterwards.

DOMINICK (*slightly thrown*) Yes, of course.

They stare at each other. She stifles a giggle, touches the top of his suit.

JANE Your suit is very peculiar, on close inspection. How do you get it off?

He deftly removes the jacket.

Very sexy, I must get some for the shop.

27 Jane's Flat. Next Morning

Sunlight through the curtains, and morning sounds. A milkman clattering, a dog barking, birds singing.
Dominick wakes with a start. He sees the time – eight thirty five – springs up in panic.

JANE Darling?
DOMINICK I'm too late.
JANE But . . . it's Saturday. Don't you ever get weekends off?

No answer.

Change your job, Gilbey?

DOMINICK I cannot.
JANE Well . . . ring them up. Tell them you're sick, you've got flu. I'll do it for you. I'll pretend I'm your landlady.
DOMINICK They wouldn't believe you.
JANE Who's they? Is it Aunt Mavis? Is she the Head of the Secret Service?
DOMINICK Yes.

Tracked 48
No Signature

Delivered By

Postage Paid GB

R37	C24	Large Letter
		750g

08-000 3BB C56

TQ 7034 9422 0GB

DAVID SHEPARD
15 NORTH STREET
DOVER
CT17 9QX

Return Address
29 Carclew Street
Truro
TR1 2DZ

MARKETPLACE SELLER

Post by the end of
06.03.2025

Paid and printed from
eBay Simple Delivery

Royal Mail: UK's lowest average parcel carbon footprint 200g CO2e

JANE   Really?
DOMINICK   Yes. Goodbye.
JANE   Wait, you must have some breakfast.
DOMINICK   No. Thank you.
JANE   Look I'll drive you . . . when will I see you again?
DOMINICK   (*going to the door*) After this, I've no idea.
JANE   Don't I even get a kiss?

But he's gone.

28 The Fairground

Dominick is running – then stops abruptly.
The fair has gone.
Brian, an elderly fairground attendant, is the only one left, picking up litter.

DOMINICK   Where is it? Where's my saucer? Where's the fair?
BRIAN   You're too late, guvnor. They've moved on to fresh pastures.
DOMINICK   What do you mean? Where have they gone?
BRIAN   Herne Bay.
DOMINICK   Herne Bay! When are they coming back?
BRIAN   Couldn't say. Depends on business, the weather . . . could be down there a couple of months. Never tell with Harry Shoe. You've only just missed 'em. They had trouble gettin' your saucer on the lorry. Look, there she goes now!

Dominick sees his flying saucer making stately progress over a flyover on the back of a lorry.

DOMINICK   I must get it back. Where's Herne Bay?
BRIAN   Kent Coast. Beside the silvery sea.

29 Jane's Flat

Loud knocking on the door. Jane opens it.
Dominick stands before her, trying to seem calm.

DOMINICK   Are you busy today?
JANE   No . . .
DOMINICK   I thought we might go to Herne Bay. Beside the silvery sea.

30 Outskirts of Herne Bay

Dominick sits beside Jane in the slowest form of transport he has ever known – her battered old car. They pass a fair as the saucer is lifted, none too carefully, off the lorry.

JANE Look, a fair! Do you like fairs, Gilbey?
DOMINICK Yes, I wish to go to it.
JANE (*happily*) Go later.

She drives on.

DOMINICK What's that smell?
JANE I need a new exhaust.

But Dominick is smelling the sea for the first time.
Montage of sea images, rolling surf.
Dominick appears over sand dunes, staring at the sea in delight and wonder – Jane takes his arm.
Jane emerges from a swim – past Dominick who is tentatively dipping his feet in.
She grabs a towel, laughing.

JANE Go for a swim, coward!
DOMINICK (*retreating*) Not in there!
JANE Why not? It's gorgeous.

They lie together among the dunes, contended and revived.

JANE You really in hot water for not going back?
DOMINICK Trouble. Yes.
JANE Worth it, isn't it? Day by the sea with me?

She tickles his face with a strand of grass.

DOMINICK Beautiful. You're all beautiful, you, Jim, Midge, Felix, Harry Shoe . . .
JANE Harry who?
DOMINICK Another friend of mine.

He changes his position to face her.

DOMINICK You're always asking the questions. Who are you? Where do you come from? What do you wish of life?
JANE My name is Jane Winters. I come from Nottingham. I'm on the retreat from a messy love affair. In hiding. And all I wish for, at the moment, is a day like this, my shop to

	stay in business – and a bloke who doesn't keep running out on me. Not much to ask for, is it?
DOMINICK	Jim Bone will not run out on you.
JANE	(*dismissively*) Jim Bone is a nice, friendly irresponsible slob.
DOMINICK	Slob? What's that?
JANE	(*annoyed*) Sometimes I think you do it deliberately! It doesn't add to your mystery. It simply infuriates, Gilbey!
DOMINICK	I promise to tell you everything soon.
JANE	What's wrong with now?
DOMINICK	We have to go to the fair now.

He gets up, grabs her hand: she resists, but he is resolute, leads her over the dunes back to the car.

31 The Fairground. Early Evening

Dominick and Jane finish a ride on a stately merry-go-round.
Dominick is feeling sick, as Jane brings him a hot dog.
They try the shooting range – Jane's very inaccurate, but Dominick hits the bull each time and wins her a giant teddy bear, and presents it to her with ceremony.
They approach the saucer – lights sparkling – attended by Harry, and surrounded by a large crowd.

HARRY   All right, don't push, one at a time . . . *don't* try and get the lid off. You can't see inside because it's genuine. Might fly off with you in it. What, lady? We found it up in Scotland, on an island. Birdwatchers spotted it . . and not one, not two but three little green men . . . here's a picture of them.

Holds up a large picture of three green men.

HARRY   I kid you not, sir. They stand three feet high, so they weren't hard to nab. They're in a special sanatorium undergoin' tests in a remote part of the Isle of Man at the moment. (*Incredulous laughter and cries of 'rubbish'*) Would I lie to you, sir? What? They've let us borrow it, they're quite friendly little geezers. But we have to keep poppin' it back to 'em for a check-up. That's our part of the bargain. So make the most of it. It may not be here tomorrow.

JANE   (*laughs*) Almost as implausible as you.

DOMINICK You're right. Come on.

Starts leading her away, but Harry has spotted them.

HARRY Hey Gilbey ...

Fights his way through the crowds.

JANE How does he know you?
DOMINICK It's Harry Shoe. Wait here. Wait!

He joins Harry – out of Jane's hearing.

DOMINICK Why did you move it? Without telling me!
HARRY Yeah, all right, I'm just goin' to explain if you give me a chance. You wasn't there.
DOMINICK I leave tonight with it. It may be the last you see of me.
HARRY Now calm down ... I went to a lot of trouble gettin' it here. It nearly fell off in Maidstone. We picked up a dozen cars followed us all the way down. Look, forget Barney, I'll give you two hundred nicker down for it and the rest in percentage ...
DOMINICK Not possible. It's mine and it stays mine, Harry.

Jane sees Harry press wads of notes into Dominick's hands. He takes some, then shakes Harry off and returns to Jane.
Harry waves his fist, infuriated.
He sees her expression: she looks suddenly depressed.

DOMINICK What problem?
JANE You came here to find Harry Shoe.
DOMINICK Yes. He's a friend.
JANE What did he give you money for? Is he a paymaster for MI5?
DOMINICK What?
JANE Or do you rob banks together?
DOMINICK I don't understand. We're having a beautiful day.
JANE (*walking away*) Doesn't do much for a girl's morale, Gilbey, to know she's just being used for a free ride to Herne Bay!
DOMINICK Stop! I only want to be with you. Like last night ... I have feelings for you that are unaccustomed to me.
JANE What do you mean, unaccustomed? Why don't you talk properly? Where did you go to school!
DOMINICK I was educated ... in Alperton, actually.
JANE Oh that accounts for it!

She walks away.

DOMINICK Jane!
JANE I'm going back to London.
DOMINICK No, we . . . No . . . stay with me tonight, please . . We can find somewhere to sleep.

Dominick looks round desperately.

JANE Bit noisy round here, not much privacy . . . (*forced to smile*) Of course we could have a dirty weekend in a Guest House.
DOMINICK Yes!

He takes her arm, and they are briefly reconciled.

32 A Guest House Bedroom. Night

We see Tretchikoff's painting, 'The Weeping Rose, above the bed in which Dominick and Jane are making ecstatic love.
At dawn, Jane is woken by the sound of gulls and breakers. She looks round and sees a note pinned on the teddy bear on Dominick's pillow.
Dominick has gone.
The note reads 'Goodbye, Jane. Please accept quids. Thank you, love Gilbey'. And a kiss.
She picks up three fivers and stares at them in startled disbelief.

33 The Cartwheel

Dominick walks along the corridor towards the mirror face-scan, and steels himself for the bad reception.
The door opens. He walks on through into the reception area.
Alaric doesn't even look up.

ALARIC Pleasant weekend?
DOMINICK I lost my saucer. It was driven away on a lorry. You been waiting since yesterday?
ALARIC Yes.
DOMINICK Apology. Has Magi called me for Caleb? I found her great-great grandmother, but not my relative. Shall I go straight in to Caleb? I'm ready for it.
ALARIC Caleb? He's on his annual flip. Observing Moses and the ten commandments. You took your chance on that, didn't you?

DOMINICK (*laughs with relief*) You mean he knows nothing?
ALARIC Not unless I report you. (*See empty container*) No rose? Ava spoke to me.
DOMINICK What did you tell her?
ALARIC What could I tell her? I don't know what you do when you land. But she's a female. Not stupid.
DOMINICK I must go home to her.
ALARIC Dominick . . . quest over. No more landings. Check?

Dominick hesitates.

I thought I'd lost you.

Dominick leaves.

34 Dominick's Home

DOMINICK Ava?

No reply – he looks into the bedroom.
Ava is in bed. She turns slowly to him, as if in a dream.

Are you unwell?
AVA I don't know, I couldn't get up.

He touches her shoulder, concerned.

Expected not to see you again.
DOMINICK Machine fault. I couldn't make the double return. No danger.

He stoops to kiss her.
She avoids him, and gets up.

AVA I'll make breakfast. I feel better.

Dominick follows Ava into the main room, then sees the container with the dust of the rose in it. He picks it up.

DOMINICK Ava?

No answer.

You opened it.

She is giving small convulsive sobs, her back to him.
He puts down the box.

You wanted to share it. I understand. I have more to

share with you. Have you even been to the sea? Smelt the sea? I want to take you now.

AVA (*turns*) The sea?

She comes past him, wiping a tear from her eye.

Cornwall, Soo.

After a moment, the Cornish coast appears on the screen with pounding waves, and gulls' cries.

There you are.

DOMINICK No, it's not the same! You have to put your feet in the water. Feel the power against your legs.

AVA The sea is dirty, Dominick. It's full of bacteria and dead fish. We are forbidden to step in it.

DOMINICK There are still visits made, to Cornwall.

AVA You are not encouraged to leave the Observation Towers and you have to book in advance.

DOMINICK (*animated*) Then do it for us. Book us a visit. You work for ThomCook!

AVA There's no reason. We have it here. No advantage.

DOMINICK I lay on a beach today. At a place called Herne Bay. I will take you there. To the same beach. And make love to you. We'll feel the sand beneath our bodies, and hear the waves and the birds above us. And we will breathe the air.

Ava drops the breakfast.
He tidies it up for her.
She sits and stares at the sea for a moment – then removes it with a dismissive wave, Soo reading her signal.
Pause.

AVA Soo . . .?
SOO Yes, Ava.
DOMINICK No, Soo.

Silence.

She can't help. You smelt the rose.

He takes her tenderly into his arms, kisses her, finding new sensations of touch in her body.
She can't respond. She feels completely disorientated and makes a token effort to push him away.

AVA It's not . . . right. I'm not composed.

DOMINICK You shouldn't be. That's our fault.
AVA You learn this with another female. I know. Tell me her name. Describe her to me.

For the first time she feels a strange pang of jealousy – and he feels guilt.

DOMINICK She is different. You are not rivals.
AVA But you . . . make love?
DOMINICK Yes.
AVA Is it different?
DOMINICK I'll show you.

*Gently he starts to undress her, kissing her Jane-style.
She moves to protest.*

DOMINICK Be still . . . still . . .
AVA I have to shower . . .
DOMINICK No you don't.

*Move close on Ava – as she leans back, closing her eyes, giving in to the new sensations in her body.
The camera pans slowly from Ava to the rose-petal dust in the container.*

35 The Pub

*Midge, Felix, Jim – and Jane, a little apart from them – are considering Gilbey's callous behaviour.
Midge is complaining about her own relationship with Felix.*

MIDGE Men are absolute bastards!
JIM (*draining his glass*) The dregs!
MIDGE (*fury*) He left her money! On the pillow.
FELIX (*looking up*) How much?
MIDGE Fifteen quid, the pig!

*Jane says nothing, sips her drink.
Dominick is looking over London from his saucer, desperate to land but heeding Alaric's warning, he turns back into space.*

36 Dominick's Home

Ava sits in middle of sofa, talking to Alaric, whose face appears on the screen.

AVA He's still landing on the flip side? I know about it. And about the woman. I'm not concerned. But he cannot find his relative so there's no reason to land. I think of his safety and Caleb knowing.

ALARIC It's over. He has not landed for weeks. Accepts it. No trouble. (*Ava smiles in relief*) I have a new partner. I am satisfied at last. Ava meet

The video camera shows Alaric's new partner.

ALARIC Haruld!

An attractive young man smiles and waves his hand in greeting to Ava.

37 The Pub, some weeks later

On the pub's TV there is a documentary about flying saucer sightings, watched by Felix, Midge, Jim, Jane – and Gordon, an old man, who is filling in his football pools.

JIM One seen in Battersea the other week. True. Young couple saw it parked on a bit of wasteland. Saw it take off. It was in the Daily Mirror.
FELIX They don't exist.
MIDGE Don't be stupid, of course they exist.
FELIX They just feed man's cretinous desire for mystery.
JANE Like God?
FELIX Like God. God exists solely to relieve us of our own banality.
MIDGE What tripe, look what's that, for God's sake!

Midge points dramatically to a flying saucer on TV.
Dominick has also seen it. He has just come in. He looks briefly alarmed.
The gang haven't yet seen him. He buys five pints.

GORDON Stenhousemuir and Cowdenbeath . . . what do you think, boys?
JIM Pardon?
GORDON Will they draw?
FELIX Not in a million years.
GORDON I'll put 'em down then.

Jane sees Dominick and for a moment thinks she's dreaming.
Then he turns and smiles and brings the drinks over on a tray.

INTENSIVE CARE

MIDGE Gilbey!
FELIX (*eyes the drinks*) Sit down. Move up, Midge.
JIM We thought the KGB had nabbed you.
DOMINICK Hello. Hello, Jane.
JANE (*cool*) Hello, Gilbey.
JIM Cheers, Gilbey. Good to see you again.
MIDGE Yes.
DOMINICK (*glancing at Jane*) Bottoms up!

They all drink.

GORDON What do you think about Scunthorpe and Rochdale?
JIM Not a lot.
DOMINICK (*interested*) What's he doing?
MIDGE Trying to become a millionaire. (*Dominick looks puzzled*) Football pools. Trying to predict the results, Gilbey.
GORDON Reckon they're good for a draw. (*puts his cross*)
FELIX What 'll you do with the winnings, Gordon? Build yourself a fall-out shelter?
MIDGE God you are depressing.
FELIX What else can he do? We're all going up.

He mimes a big bang.

DOMINICK No you're not.
FELIX You seriously think we'll get through the next five years without a big bang?

Dominick glances at Jane, wanting to warn her.

DOMINICK There will be a war, in 1999.
JIM That's what Nostrodamus says!
DOMINICK You must be out of London then.
JANE Where will you be?
DOMINICK (*smiles*) Cannot predict. But London will recover. South America won't. But London will. Rayners Lane will still exist.
MIDGE Where do you get your information?
GORDON Bugger . . . broke my pencil.
JIM (*as Dominick hesitates*) Little green men in flying saucers.
DOMINICK I guess like you, of course. But I see a bright future. Some things lost. But Felix and Midge will have a home and live with credits.
MIDGE Live in credit? Him?
DOMINICK And have babies. (*smiles at Midge*)

Jane gets up abruptly.

JANE / Must get back to the flat.
DOMINICK / I want to talk to you.
JANE / What about, Gilbey?

Jane goes to the door. He follows quickly.

DOMINICK / Jane?

Jane hurries back to the shop with Dominick in pursuit. He accidently kicks the brake off a stationary push chair. It starts to run towards the road. A truck is passing. Dominick stops and stares frozen in horror: in slow motion, he sees the mother straining, running to catch her child, the truck bearing down. The brakes screech and the driver leaps out. The mother grabs the baby from the pushchair unhurt and as it starts bawling, hugs it. The driver returns the pushchair, mother and baby to the pavement. Dominick stumbles back into a doorway, sweating.
Jane has seen the commotion, comes back and finds herself physically having to support Dominick who is now sweating and shivering.

JANE / What happened?
DOMINICK / Accident.
JANE / Come on, Gilbey. (*she leads him away*)

38 Jane's Flat. Evening

Dominick drinks tea, surrounded by three growing kittens and their mother Merle.

JANE / Better? (*he nods*) What did you have to say to me?
DOMINICK / The truth. Will you trust me?
JANE / Don't know if I can, Gilbey. You've made a pretty big fool of me.
DOMINICK / I love you.
JANE / Funny way of showing it.
DOMINICK / I have no choice. I come from the future, from the year two thousand one hundred and thirty. I came in a saucer.

She starts laughing, turns away, he is forced to plunge on, regardless of the mounting absurdity of his tale.

DOMINICK / I have work as a Coro, a Correspondent. I make reports on London Transport. I leave my saucer in a fairground. You saw it in Herne Bay. I have to keep leaving . . . to return. Landing is forbidden. A man called Cochrane. Teddy Cochrane landed in Ohio, US ... he killed a dog and changed history. I nearly killed a child. I would have done the same. I take terrible risks to see you. But you give me so much life, vitality which I take back. So much that we've lost. You're my gift to my own people ... are you listening?

She has sunk onto a pile of clothes, her head buried away from him. He thinks she is still laughing.

DOMINICK The reason I was absent ... my partner-mechanic who arranges my landing refused to do it again. And the fair was in Herne Bay! I couldn't find a safe place ... until today when I saw it return to London. And decided to see you once more, to say goodbye and explain.

She swings round at him, he sees her face drenched in tears.

JANE (*angry*) You expect me to believe that! You really seriously expect me to believe ... I don't know what your game is, Gilbey ... you can be the man in the moon for all I care! Just don't insult me! Just go away from here and don't ever come back, please! Get in your Saucer and bugger off!

Dominick is at a loss.

DOMINICK I took your rose back. I gave it ...
JANE Oh Christ, Gilbey!
DOMINICK (*helpless*) I still live in Rayners Lane ...

Jane hurls some clothes at him. He ducks.

DOMINICK It's the truth!
JANE Truth? You want the truth? The truth is I'm pregnant! I'm carrying your child! How does that affect the future Gilbey? Any comforting theories for that?

Dominick is horrified.

39 Caleb's Office

Caleb is calmly pouring tea.
Dominick has just blurted out the terrible news, and stands ashen-faced.

CALEB Naturally we knew what you were doing. Alaric was

permitted to give you every assistance. Will you take tea? It can be most reviving in stress.

Dominick takes the tea with a trembling hand.

CALEB   What pleases me is my reading of your character, Dominick. All reports indicated your penchant for adventure. What surprises me is your tardiness in realising your mission. You landed to locate your ancestor. (*Dominick is slowly realising*) That's right, he's you. Dominick Hide. It happens to one in a million. A genetic time-slip. When we are able, we correct it. Your great grandfather was born in the Portobello sector of London, in 1981. Or should have been. And now will be. I congratulate you on your enterprise and I rely on your discretion.

DOMINICK   The risks ... Cochrane ...

CALEB   We took minimal chance on that. We scanned ahead, though we could not foresee everything ... there appeared to be no catastrophe in your wake.

DOMINICK   I must see her. To provide for her and my son. Once more.

CALEB   Not granted ... officially. (*he smiles*) But that seems not to have obstructed you up to now.

Dominick nods, smiles his thanks, finishes the tea and goes to the door.

CALEB   Dominick. (*he turns*) Do come back. Won't you?

He nods, goes.

40 Jane's Flat

Jane, five months pregnant, is drying her hair in the bathroom. The door bell rings. She goes to answer it, and sees a doorful of red roses topped by a priest's hat.
The roses are lowered to reveal Dominick, grinning.

DOMINICK   Delivery for Miss Winters?

JANE   (*not too friendly*) You're four months early. Come in.

DOMINICK   Where shall I put them?

JANE   What are they for, Gilbey?

DOMINICK   They're for my great-great grandmother.

JANE   (*annoyed*) Shove 'em in the sink.

He does.

DOMINICK Shall I make coffee?
JANE No thank you.

Dominick comes to the door and grins at her. He has some newspapers under his arm.

DOMINICK Are you well? You look beautiful.
JANE (*sighs*) Yes I suppose ... all things considering ... actually I'm not sleeping too well. I have nightmares. Sometimes I almost believe what you told me.
DOMINICK What I have to tell you now ... you must believe. It was all calculated, my return. Our meeting. It was designed. Our son will continue the family line until it finally reaches me.
JANE (*sitting, confused*) Son? Definitely a boy?
DOMINICK Oh yes. What are these going to be? (*picks up her knitting*).
JANE Booties, but I've rather lost heart.
DOMINICK Don't. We have work to do. You make pools, don't you?
JANE I've grown out of that, Gilbey.

Dominick is puzzled. She gets up, sorts through bills and fishes out a Littlewoods coupon.

JANE You mean these sort of pools? Or jacuzzis.
DOMINICK These. (*talking them*)
JANE They send them each week but I don't bother with them.
DOMINICK You must. I don't understand. (*hands her the paper*) Read the results.
JANE But ... it's Monday.
DOMINICK (*smiles*) No it isn't. It's next Sunday. Look.
JANE Oh God.
DOMINICK I picked them up from the corner of the street an hour ago.
JANE How?
DOMINICK Landed. Got the papers. Took off again. Came back today. (*she has to laugh*) We want the best for our son, don't we? Fill them in. Go on.
JANE It's cheating.
DOMINICK What's cheating mean?

She starts filling in the coupons, her spirits suddenly reviving.

JANE Can I tell the others?
DOMINICK No. But you can provide for them.
JANE Don't think I need to provide for Jim. He's fallen on his feet. Marketing your hats.

DOMINICK Yes I saw some people wearing them when I was buying the papers.
JANE They're catching on. It's been a hot summer and there've been scares in the press about the sun breaking through the ozone layer or something. Nottingham Forest Nil, Stoke City Four. That's impossible!
DOMINICK Wait and see.
JANE Is it all really true? (*he nods*) Saucers aren't from other planets?
DOMINICK No, people from other planets come in different containers, like the Number Fifteen bus!
JANE (*laughs*) So much I want to know.
DOMINICK No – it's best if you know nothing. (*she nods*)
JANE I think you should know that Jim asked me to marry him and I turned him down. (*smiles*) Oh you probably know that already.
DOMINICK No, I won't spy on you.
JANE Will I ever marry – if I can't marry you?
DOMINICK It's not for me to say.
JANE How long have we got together?
DOMINICK Until tonight. When the fair closes.
JANE I promise I'll believe everything, if you let me see you take off.
DOMINICK Finish the pools.

She continues to write.
We leave them together, domesticated for the last time.

41 The Fairground. Night

It's closing down, lights are being switched off. Jane and Dominick walk among the stragglers.
It's a bitter-sweet moment. Small boys are playing near the saucer.

JANE You'll miss him growing up. Can't you break the rules again? (*he shakes his head*) Suppose I came with you?
DOMINICK I have another female.
JANE Naturally. What's her name?
DOMINICK Ava.
JANE Couldn't we all live together?
DOMINICK I'd have to keep you in a snaptight container. Or you'd die.

They arrive at the saucer.

JANE (*laughing*) Sorry but I really can't believe you're seriously going to take off in that.
DOMINICK (*serious*) Goodbye, Jane.
JANE (*in sudden panic*) Don't go.

She clings to him hugging him tightly.
He gently releases himself. The saucer is now clear of people.

JANE I love you.
DOMINICK (*smiles and waves*) I love you. Be a good mother.
JANE (*as he goes*) What shall I call him? Gilbey?
DOMINICK Dominick. Dominick Hide.

She watches him climb into the saucer and close the lid, but she still can't believe it.
The saucer's lights change and it begins to hum, then gently eases away. Jane raises her head, watching the last wisp of the saucer trailing off into the night sky.

BRIAN (*who is standing beside her*) It's to do with Maggie and the Russians. Top secret.
JANE Yes . . . yes I know . . .

She looks back at the sky with tears in her eyes.

42 The Beach. Day

Breakers are rolling in and there are two people on the sand: Jane, with a cine camera, and a boy – Dominick's son, aged eight – who is building a sandcastle.
The boy is wearing a T-shirt with 'Olympics 1988' on it.
Then he takes it off, and throws it down. It lies there as we saw it when Mavis was showing the film.
We track in over Jane's shoulder to see exactly the same piece of film now that we saw earlier. But this time we hear dialogue over the sound of the sea.

JANE What's that room?
BOY (*pointing to the top of the castle*) That's daddy's room. Why did he go away?
JANE He had no choice.
BOY Was he a good man?
JANE He was a man in a million.

Her voice drifts away as the camera leaves them slowly and begins a three hundred and sixty degree pan over the sea on its journey to another part of the beach.
There we see Dominick, Ava, and their baby in a peculiar futuristic carrycot.
Dominick is stomping about in the shallows, laughing and splashing.
Ava laughs at his antics, as Jane used to laugh.
We continue panning past them towards the point of departure.
The beach is now empty, the sandcastle gone.
No Jane, no young Dominick. Just emptiness and evening sunlight, and gulls' cries swelling over laughter.

Looking for Vicky

by Jane Hollowood

An Introduction by Jane Hollowood

When I was eight years old, finding myself alone in the house, I plucked up courage to make my first ever phone call. I dialled the operator (in the 1950s, in country districts, you had to ask the exchange to get your number) only to hear a stern voice telling me that no calls could be made from my house because we *hadn't paid our phone bill!* It sounds funny now, but at the time I was struck dumb with terror and shame. I felt like a criminal. I didn't dare touch the phone again for years.

Thinking about it, maybe this trivial childhood incident provided the germ of the idea for this play, *Looking for Vicky*. It gave me the idea that the telephone can, in certain circumstances, be scary, even menacing. After all, you never know who is lurking at the other end of the line, and if you are alone in a remote house, as Clare is in the play, even the ring of the telephone, suddenly breaking the silence, can make you jump.

With this theme in mind, I set out to write a thriller about frightening phone calls. Once into the writing, however, the play quickly became about a lot of other things as well; about loneliness, about feeling vulnerable, about the relationship between mothers and daughters, about growing up and becoming attractive, about growing older and losing your attraction.

There are three main characters: Clare, the mother, Philippa, her fourteen year old daughter, and Red, Philippa's secret lover. The story is set in London commuter country, in the pleasant wooded hills of Surrey. Each day Derek, the father, sets off for his office in the City, Philippa and the two other children go to school, and Clare is left alone. The dishwasher and washing machine whirr, the goldfish swim round the ornamental pond, the birds sing and Clare, on her own in this middle class paradise, is supposed to lead (as husband Derek frequently tells her) 'the life of Riley'. Except that she doesn't. She hates it. To her the house has become a prison.

The trouble is, she hasn't got enough to do. She hasn't got a job and, being new to the district, she hasn't got any friends yet. Her only purpose in life seems to be to wait hand and foot on an ungrateful family.

Like most people with not enough to interest them, she's discontented. She resents her husband's busy working life, she's jealous of Philippa's social life, but she's so lacking in confidence that she can't get any life going for herself. She feels herself to be unattractive (even though she's only in her thirties, she dresses like a middle-aged woman) and above all, she feels *vulnerable*. Everything about her life in the country seems to threaten her; the neighbour's dogs, the telephone men, the roadman, even the sound of the birds singing. And so of course when something *really* does threaten her, when Red phones, she is terrified.

Philippa, her daughter, is a very different sort of character. She sees clearly the trap her mother has fallen into, and she's determined to avoid it. She's going to be tough. She's going to be like the girl she has invented, Miss Vicky le Fleming . . . artistic, free, glamorous, independent. But for all her rebellious ways, Philippa is also vulnerable. Otherwise why does she tell both her mother and her boyfriend a pack of lies?

Red is a more shadowy figure. In a way he is all *image*. The big motorbike, the way he speaks and stands, his clothes, they all speak of someone who fancies himself as a James Dean sort of character, a rebel without a cause. OK, so he's got no job. OK, so he's been kicked out of his lodgings. See if he cares. He can manage.

But watch him closely. See him waking up, shivering and scared after a night sleeping rough. Note how desperate he is to track down his girl friend Vicky. Once he's in trouble he badly needs her help. He's not quite the macho man he'd like us to think he is. He too is vulnerable. He needs someone to lean on. And when he can't lean on Vicky because she doesn't exist, she's only a fourteen year old schoolgirl called Philippa, he quickly turns to Clare, her mother. Suddenly she seems a much better bet.

On one level the play remains the mystery story I set out to write. On another, it becomes a play about the confident images people present, and the uncertainties that lie beneath. Comfortable middle class Clare, who has everything, longs for love. Outsider Red longs for security. Rebellious Philippa, experimenting with sex, bored stiff by her home and her parents, is still much more of a child than she thinks.

By the end of the play, the characters have revealed these layers to us and, through the unravelling of the mystery, have learnt to understand themselves and each other a bit better. In particular, the central relationship, between Clare and Philippa, will never be quite the same again. Ditched by Red and with her silly deception humiliatingly unmasked, Philippa realises at last how well her mother understands her, how close the bond between them still is.

Clare, first through conquering her fear of Red, then through the flattering discovery that he finds her desireable, finally through her reconciliation with her daughter, comes to see that she is still a woman, a sexual being, a person with something to offer. She needn't be a dowdy has-been. She can assert herself. She can stand up for herself, as indeed she does when Derek comes home from work that night. Who knows, maybe she will actually get herself a job, step back into the swim of things, start enjoying herself.

The only person in the play who does not reveal himself is Derek. With him, image and self seem to be one and the same thing. It looks as if he will go to the grave worrying about telephone extensions and tomorrow's meetings in the office, swinging his imaginary squash racket in practice shots as he waits for Clare to run him to the station, entirely unaware of how those around him are really feeling. Poor old Derek. He can't be quite as simple as that. Maybe we need to explore *his* inner world in another play.

Looking for Vicky was first shown on television in 1980 as part of an Independent Television drama series called ITV Playhouse. It was made by Thames Television and produced by John Bowen, who gave me invaluable help and advice in the final shaping of the script, and taught me many important things about the craft of writing for television.

Jane Hollowood, July 1987

The Cast

Clare Watkins (late 30's, middle-class)
Polly (her younger daughter, age 12)
James (her son, age 10)
Derek (her husband, about 40, works in the City)
Philippa (her older daughter, age 14)
A roadman (oldish, could be thought menacing)
Red (age 19, working-class, unemployed, punk-rocker)
Mrs Price-Williams (elderly Welsh lady, previous owner of the house)
Voice of a telephone operator
Greengrocer (middle-aged)
Eric ⎫
     ⎬ (two young workmen)
Fred ⎭
Voice of a lady on a radio phone-in
Voice of the interviewer conducting the phone-in

Looking for Vicky

Part One

The house is set in commuter country, in the Surrey hills, among pines and rhododendrons. It is a summer morning: hear birdsong, the cuckoo, the gentle rustle of leaves.
The window is open, and through it comes the noise of a family preparing for the day – the clatter of dishes on a draining board, the radio, a child playing the recorder, doors banging. And also voices:

CLARE Twenty past! Get your things! Put your recorder *away*, Polly. Hurry up.
DEREK Anyone seen my hat?
POLLY Can I take an apple?
DEREK Has anyone seen my *hat*?
CLARE Philippa! Phi ... lip ... pa!

The front door opens, and Clare appears, wearing canary yellow linen trousers and a head scarf firmly knotted under the chin. She is followed by Polly and James (dressed for school) and Derek in a dark suit, with hat and briefcase. He carries a squash racket. Clare hurries the children into the car, gets into the driver's seat.
Derek pauses, looks around in satisfaction, breathes the morning air, and plays a couple of imaginary squash shots.

DEREK Fantastic day!

He gets into the passenger seat, as Clare beeps the horn for the last child.

DEREK What are you doing today, darling? Don't go out, will you? Remember the telephone men are coming.

Clare gives him a cold look.
Philippa comes out of the front door, and stops to do up her shoes,

taking her time. She is in school uniform, with her hair scraped back in a bunch.

CLARE Come on. Daddy'll miss his train.

Philippa walks slowly to the car.

CLARE Do hurry up.
PHILIPPA All right, all right. No need to get into a flap.

She gets in, and slams the door. Clare starts the car a shade too violently, and it moves off down the drive and turns into the lane at the top.
As they drive along, an old roadman salutes them from the ditch in which he is scything grass. They ignore him. Light glints on the blade of his scythe.
Meanwhile, in the hall, the telephone is ringing, and no one is there to answer.

Half an hour later. The car comes back. Clare gets out. She stands and looks about. She hears the blackbird's song, and makes a face; her attitude to living in isolated conditions in the country is not the same as her husband's. She goes into the kitchen. This is a small room with an open window, which looks out up the drive, and has the sink below. There is a dresser, a fridge, a washing-machine, a dishwasher, a notice board. The dining table is littered with cornflake packets and dirty breakfast dishes. She takes off her headscarf. It is very quiet, so that sounds are exaggerated. A clock ticks. She pulls on washing up gloves with a rubbery snap.
The phone rings in the hall.
She jumps. The phone rarely rings in that house during the day. She goes to answer it. Above the phone is a mirror. She looks into it, touches her hair, clears her throat, picks up the phone. Puts on her 'telephone voice'.

CLARE Blackwood 235.

Pips are heard, then a man's voice, flat, expressionless, distanced by the phone.

VOICE (RED) Vicky, please.
CLARE I'm sorry?
VOICE I want to speak to Vicky.
CLARE I think you must have the wrong number. Sorry.

She puts down the phone, and goes back into the kitchen, but the phone rings again. She picks it up wearily.

CLARE Blackwood 235.
VOICE (RED) That's right. I want to speak to Vicky.
CLARE I'm sorry. You've got the same wrong number.
VOICE What number is that?
CLARE Blackwood 235.
VOICE Then I want to speak to Vicky.
CLARE (*patiently*) I'm sorry. There's no Vicky here. You must have the wrong number.

She replaces the receiver, and goes back to the kitchen. The phone rings again. She picks up the phone, and says very strongly:

CLARE Blackwood 235.

Pips go.

CLARE I've told you it's a wrong number.
VOICE Can I speak to Vicky, please.
CLARE Look, what number are you trying to get?
VOICE Blackwood 235. It's here. I got it written down on a piece of paper.
CLARE Sorry. I am Blackwood 235, but there's nobody here called Vicky. You must have written the number down wrong. (*She pauses, then says sharply*) Hello?
VOICE Could I speak to Vicky?
CLARE I told you. She doesn't live here. You've got the wrong number. Goodbye.

She slams down the phone, and goes back into the kitchen. She is vexed. It shows in the way she puts dishes into the dishwasher, adds soap and switches it on.
The phone rings again. She will not answer it. She is determined. She wipes surfaces obsessively. The phone continues to ring, she gives up, goes into the hall to answer it. Just as she reaches it, it stops ringing. She is on way back to the kitchen, when it rings again. Very angrily, she picks it up.

CLARE Look I've told you —

She is interrupted by the noise of the pips, and realises she hasn't been heard so far, so she has to start again.

CLARE Look, I've told you this is the wrong number. Will you please stop bothering me?
VOICE Top flat. Come on. She lives in the top flat.
CLARE We're not flats. We're a private house. There's no top flat.
VOICE You can't be bovvered to fetch her. That's the trouble, innit? You can't be bovvered to fetch her.
CLARE It's not a question of fetching anyone; there's no one to fetch. I'm the only person in the house.
VOICE Who are you? Are you new there or something?
CLARE Look here. It doesn't matter who I am. The point is . . .

The pips go. The phone clicks back to a dialling tone. Clare hesitates, then replaces the receiver.

CLARE Well, we *are* new, I suppose.

There is a telephone-address-book by the phone. She takes off a rubber glove, and picks up the book to look for the phone number of the previous owners of the house. The phone rings.
She picks it up, waits for the pips, and says:

CLARE Look, I've been thinking. I think you must want the Price-Williams. I'm afraid they moved away six months ago. We're the new people here, but I do have their number somewhere if you'd like it.
VOICE I dunno what you're talking about.
CLARE Just let me give you this number. It may be –
VOICE I've got to speak to her. It's urgent.
CLARE I'm trying to help you.
VOICE Don't put me on. I ain't got no more money. Just go and get Vicky, will you?
CLARE I've got their number here somewhere. I may have to put the phone down to find it.

She begins to flap, trying to turn the pages, and drops the phone.

VOICE (*indignant*) You're playing bloody games with me. You –

The pips go, and the voice is cut off. Clare puts the phone down, shaken. She stares at it. She takes off the other rubber glove, finds the Price-Williams number, dials the number, which answers.

CLARE Hullo! Is that Penzance two . . . er Mrs Price-Williams?
VOICE (*Welsh, cautious*) Yes . . .?
CLARE This is Mrs Watkins.

LOOKING FOR VICKY

VOICE Yes . . .?
CLARE Bracken Tops. We bought the house from you.
VOICE (*now reassured*) Oh, Mrs *Watkins*. Goodness, yes! And phoning all this way. My dear it's the most expensive time of day. Is something wrong?
CLARE It's about your daughter.
VOICE Helen?
CLARE Oh! . . . Helen is it? I wondered if –
VOICE She's married now, you know, living in Llandidrod Wells; they have a lovely house.
CLARE Was there ever anyone called –
VOICE – natural stone, and everything electric –
CLARE – called Vicky living here? A friend, perhaps?
VOICE No, dear, Llandidrod Wells. A professional man, an accountant, she married. Persuaded my husband to put in one of those clocks, you know, on the telephone; it tells you how much the call is costing; you'd never imagine how it ticks up. I never use the telephone myself nowadays for outgoing calls. That's why it's such a pleasure, you see, if somebody like yourself –

And so it goes on, while Clare holds the phone away from herself and looks upstairs.

CLARE Top flat? There's never been a top flat.

Later the same morning. Outside the village shop the greengrocer is helping Clare carry boxes of groceries to the car.

CLARE Thanks so much (*Pause*) I say . . .
GREENGROCER Yes?
CLARE It's nothing really. (*Embarrassed laugh*) I keep getting phone calls for someone called Vicky, and they absolutely swear they haven't got the wrong number and I just wondered if there was anyone round here called Vicky . . . or perhaps if someone in the house before us had that name . . . I wondered if you knew.
GREENGROCER Vicky? Vicky. No. No, you've got me there. The people before you, the . . .
CLARE The Price-Williams.
GREENGROCER Yes, well they did have a daughter. What was she called? Whatever was her name?
CLARE Helen.
GREENGROCER I'll just go and ask Doreen.

CLARE   Oh, please don't bother. I just thought I'd ask while I was here. It's really not at all important.

She gets into the car and drives off.
The greengrocer watches her go.
Back home she carries in big boxes of groceries, one by one, past the phone in the hall. She eyes it, daring it to ring. It doesn't.
She comes in with the third and final box. The phone rings. She hesitates, then puts down the box to answer it.

CLARE   (*wary*) Hullo?
OPERATOR   Go ahead, caller.
VOICE   Where you bin?
CLARE   Look here! I've had enough of this. Will you –
VOICE   You went out.
CLARE   Shopping. I went out shopping and . . . but it's nothing to do with you. This is a wrong number.
VOICE   Right number. I got it through the operator this time, didn't I? Can you fetch Vicky, please?
CLARE   There is nobody called Vicky living here. Nobody called Vicky ever has lived here. I don't care what is written down on your piece of paper. You have the wrong number. I am now going to put the phone down. Please don't bother me again.
VOICE   Look, you bloody tart, I –

She puts down the phone. She is shaking. She tries to pick up the box of groceries, but she's trembling so much that things are spilling. She looks at herself in the mirror by the phone. A frightened face looks back at her. She decides to leave everything where it is and go out. She decides to call on her neighbours.

She walks along the lane. Suddenly, scarily, the roadman rises out of the ditch. She is startled.

ROADMAN   Morning.
CLARE   Good morning.
ROADMAN   I see you in your car.
CLARE   (*stops reluctantly*) Yes. That's right.
ROADMAN   Howdjer like it, living up here, eh?
CLARE   Oh . . . very much. It's beautiful, isn't it?
ROADMAN   Going for a little walk?
CLARE   Just popping next door.
ROADMAN   Next door's half a mile.

LOOKING FOR VICKY

CLARE   Yes. Yes, it is, I'm afraid.
ROADMAN   On the borrow, are you? Run out of something?
CLARE   Well, no, actually . . . (*Pause*) As a matter of fact, there's a . . . there's a man been bothering me.
ROADMAN   Coming to the door, has he? You want to be careful.

Horrified, she takes a step back. The roadman suddenly seems menacing.

CLARE   Oh, no. Nothing like that. Not to the door.
ROADMAN   Can't be too careful.

She goes on quickly. He watches her, his scythe glinting.
Further down the lane she comes to an array of notices fastened to a pair of imposing gates. The entrance to her neighbours' house.

    TRESPASSERS WILL BE PROSECUTED
    GUARD DOGS
    PRIVATE
    TRADESMEN'S ENTRANCE (*with arrow*)
    BURGLAR ALARM IN PERMANENT OPERATION.

Clare touches the latch, and instantly a dog hurls itself against the gates, barking and growling. She backs away in alarm, turns and runs.

Back home Clare carries her lunch on a tray into the garden: some sliced bread, a pot of marmalade, a bottle of sherry and a glass. She settles down with the Daily Express and a large glass of sherry. The phone rings. She hurries into the house, and her paper blows into the pond. She picks up the receiver.

VOICE   You put the phone down on me. You mustn't do that. Nobody does that. I put 20 p in this time so you listen. Right?
CLARE   Is this some sort of practical joke? Is that it? A rather silly sort of joke that's gone on long after it's stopped being funny?
VOICE   Ha ha ha.
CLARE   Perhaps you're someone I know. Perhaps you're disguising your voice. Am I right? Do I know you?
VOICE   (*laughing*) You are amazing. I can't understand what you're playing at.
CLARE   I'm not playing at anything. You are.
VOICE   Could I speak to Vicky, please?
CLARE   Who's Vicky?

VOICE Vicky le Fleming.
CLARE I see. Vicky le Fleming. And where does she live?
VOICE I got the address written. Bracken Tops.

A moment. Silence. So he knows her address. She is frightened.

CLARE What did you say?
VOICE Bracken Tops.
CLARE (*trying to laugh it off*) Well, it certainly is very extraordinary. We are Bracken Tops. (*Helpless*) Look, this is some sort of joke, isn't it? Who are you really?
VOICE Shit, I've had enough of this. I'm coming round. I got the address.
CLARE Oh, no. No. You can't do that. I'm going out. I'm going out right away.
VOICE Well, if you was out, I could go up and see Vicky. Don't worry.
CLARE I absolutely forbid you to come here.

The voice laughs.

CLARE I'm warning you. If you pester me again, I shall be forced to –

She is interrupted by a loud knocking at the front door. She looks fearfully at the phone, but it can't be him. She puts down the phone and goes to answer the door.

Cut to a telephone box.
A dirty male hand, with heavy rings, one with a swastika, holds the phone, then bangs it back on the hook.

Cut to the house.
Two young workmen, Fred and Eric, are at the door. Eric has a worksheet.

FRED Mrs Watkins?
CLARE Yes?
FRED Phone, madam. We've come to do the work on your telephone.
ERIC (*consults sheet*) Resite downstairs phone, and –
FRED – put in an upstairs extension. Right?
CLARE Oh, yes! (*With relief*) I'd forgotten you were coming; I wasn't supposed to go out. Come in. Well, here is the phone at present.

It's still off the hook. She replaces it firmly.

CLARE: We want it moved through to the kitchen. I'd better just show you upstairs where the extension is to go. If you'll just follow me.

She leads the way. Eric winks at Fred. They follow.

Cut to the phone box.
Camera is the character at first. So we just see the door of the phone box open in front of us, and we approach a motor-bike which stands outside.
Change the shot. Now we see a dusty leather boot kicking the starter of the motor-bike, and hear the engine.

Back in the kitchen, Clare has brought her lunch tray in from the garden, and is standing eating, uncomfortably aware of Fred and Eric in the hall. She hears Eric laugh. She thinks they're laughing at her (they're not), and becomes more uneasy than she already was. She takes a quick swig of sherry. She looks out of the window and up the drive.

ERIC: (*heard*) You never.
FRED: (*heard*) I bloody did.

She turns to look towards the hall. What are they talking about?

ERIC: (*heard*) Well, you go in.
FRED: (*heard*) No, you go in.

She backs away, apprehensive. A knock at the door, and Eric enters.

ERIC: Excuse me.
CLARE: Yes?
ERIC: There's a bit of a problem.
CLARE: About the phone?

Pause. He looks at her.

ERIC: Right.
CLARE: What about the phone?
ERIC: It's the worksheet, you see.
CLARE: Yes?
ERIC: We've disconnected the phone. Arranged for disconnection. It's been disconnected.

CLARE Why?
ERIC Routine procedure.
CLARE But I wanted to phone my husband. There's something . . . (*Almost to herself*) Still . . . After all, you're here.
ERIC Well, that's the problem.
CLARE What is?
ERIC The cabling.
CLARE Yes?
ERIC It's the worksheet at fault. You've got a long run.
CLARE Yes?
ERIC Requiring extra cabling.
CLARE But you've disconnected the phone.
ERIC Right.

He's been carrying the disconnected phone, and now dumps it on the table.

ERIC Fred!

Fred enters.

FRED All right? (*To Clare*) Just off, then.
CLARE But you can't just go.

Fred looks at Eric. You can't trust Eric to get it right.

FRED He should've explained. It's the cabling. Additional cabling. You got a long run. It's the worksheet at fault.
CLARE But you've disconnected the phone.
FRED We have to disconnect the phone. That's the first thing. You disconnect the phone, then you begin the job. Routine procedure.
CLARE You can't leave me with the phone disconnected. I must have it.

They look at each other.

FRED (*explaining patiently*) It's the worksheet at fault.

They start moving away.

CLARE Wait! How long are you going to be?

They look at each other.

FRED About an hour. Wouldn't you say, Eric?
ERIC Shouldn't be more than that.
FRED See you later, then.

LOOKING FOR VICKY

They go out, laughing and drive away.
The clock ticks in the silence. Clare looks at the phone, its wires adrift. There is a sudden bang from somewhere in the house. She jumps, and listens. The fridge switches itself on, and buzzes. The papers on the notice-board rustle. There is another bang.

CLARE This bloody house!

She picks up her bag from the table. She's not staying.

Cut to a country road.
We see a motor-bike speeding along. We do not see more than the lower half of the body of the rider.

Outside the house, Clare is pinning a notice 'Back at four' on the door.
As she walks to the car, she hears the bang from indoors again. She looks up: it's a window. She walks on to the car, gets in, and starts up the engine.

Cut to the lane.
The roadman watches the car pass, smiling.

In a street near a school, Polly (still playing her recorder) and James are already in the back seat of the car. Clare is now collecting Philippa, who gets in the front seat.

CLARE Did you have a good day?

Philippa stares out of the window on her side.

PHILIPPA It was OK. (*Pause*) What are we waiting for?

Clare tries to start the engine. After about six tries:

CLARE Oh dear!
PHILIPPA It might help if Polly stopped playing her recorder.
JAMES Put the choke in, Mum. You're drowning it.

Polly stops playing.

POLLY Miss Roberts says we've got to practice every day.

Clare tries the engine again. No success.

CLARE Oh, Lord!
JAMES If you wait a bit, it'll dry out.
PHILIPPA Why on earth did you pull the choke out in the first place?

CLARE   I'm sorry. I wasn't thinking. It'll start in a minute. (*low voice to Philippa*) The trouble is my mind's on other things. I've had an awful day. I've been having funny phone calls. You know – someone trying to scare me.

PHILIPPA   (*makes a bored noise, then asks with urgency*) Did you wash my black jeans?

CLARE   I can't remember. I don't think I washed anything.

PHILIPPA   I've got to wear them.

CLARE   Listen, I've had a terrible day, with the telephone men, and . . . so on. I didn't get round to washing.

PHILIPPA   Honestly, I asked you specially this morning. You just didn't listen, did you? I need them for tonight, for going round to Susan's.

Clare tries the car again. It starts.

POLLY   Hurrah!

JAMES   Well done, Mum.

PHILIPPA   Could you possibly drive home reasonably quickly? I mean, a bit more than your usual twenty miles an hour.

As they drive along the lane, the roadman steps out of the ditch, waving his scythe. Clare stops, and winds down the window.

PHILIPPA   Do go *on*, Mum. Never mind him.

ROADMAN   You 'ad a caller 'bout an hour ago. Just thought I'd tell you.

CLARE   The telephone men? In a yellow van, I expect.

ROADMAN   Didn't see him too clear, I knew you were out.

CLARE   Oh? . . . Thank you.

She drives on.
The car turns in at the gate, and goes up the drive.
The figure of a man steps out from concealment in the rhododendron bushes, and stares after the car. We see his back view only, against the light.

Polly has gone back to playing the recorder. Clare is about to get the tea. Philippa comes in, and goes straight to the fridge.

CLARE   It's too bad the phone men haven't come back yet. Really the limit.

Philippa takes a fruit yoghurt from the fridge.

PHILIPPA I suppose I'll have to wear my green ones.
CLARE What are you doing? I'm just about to make the tea.

Philippa gets a spoon, and peels off the lid.

PHILIPPA I told you. I'm going round to Susan's.
CLARE Philippa, I wonder if you'd mind not going to Susan's tonight. I'd like you here.
PHILIPPA We always do our homework together.
CLARE I'm asking you just this once. Please.
PHILIPPA I've got to go. That's all there is to it.
CLARE Polly, stop playing that bloody recorder for a minute, would you, please?

Polly stops playing, and listens, interested.

CLARE Listen, tonight I'd like you to stay at home, and have your tea with the rest of us. (*Philippa finishes yoghurt, gazing absently out of the window*) Are you listening?

Philippa opens the fridge, and takes out another yoghurt.

PHILIPPA Yes.
CLARE And put that back. The others are for Polly and James.
PHILIPPA (*opens the pot*) There's plenty left. At least six.
CLARE Look, I'm not going to argue with you; I don't think I need to do that. My goodness, when I was your age, when I was fourteen, I never went out at all. Ever. (*Philippa pulls a face*) And tonight there are reasons.
PHILIPPA (*with her mouth full*) What reasons?
CLARE I told you about those phone calls. They've given me the creeps. And he threatened . . .
PHILIPPA *Threatened?*
CLARE That he'd come round here.
PHILIPPA Blimey, Mum! Honestly! (*scrapes round pot*) Everyone gets dirty phone calls. And they always threaten to come round and that.
CLARE You heard the roadman. He said someone *had* been round.
PHILIPPA (*not listening*) They're just pathetic. You should feel sorry for them. It's the only way they get their kicks.
CLARE The roadman said –
PHILIPPA Someone like you is a perfect target, of course.
CLARE What do you mean?
PHILIPPA Housewife. Home all day. I mean you'd be so easy to scare. You always blow everything up.

CLARE I see.

PHILIPPA (*cleaning round pot with fingers*) Yeah. You get things out of proportion. It's being here so much. You'd feel better if you went out and enjoyed yourself a bit more. You could still have a good time if you made the effort. (*Pause*) Susan's mother works in family planning. She says she'd die if she had to stay at home all the time.

CLARE I see.

PHILIPPA I mean, for a start your clothes – why do you wear those baggy yellow trousers all the time? Nobody wears wide trousers any more.

She throws the yoghurt pot carelessly onto the draining board.

PHILIPPA You're alway so grim. Come on. Try a smile.

Clare slaps Philippa's face.

CLARE Stop it! How dare you talk like that? How do you think I feel?

Philippa shrugs.

CLARE You can just go up to your room, and stay there, and don't come down until you're ready to apologise.

Philippa goes out, slamming the door hard. Polly begins to play her recorder again.

Later. Outside the house, the man moves away through the bushes. Then the figure of a girl climbs down the roof. She is a freaky creature, with bird's-nest hair sticking out in all directions, a mask-like face heavily made up with white on the skin, black round the eyes, purple lipstick. She wears green skintight jeans, gym shoes, a shiny silver plastic jacket, a T-shirt. She jumps to the ground, and runs off into the bushes. This is Miss Vicky le Fleming. We must not be able to recognise her as Philippa.

In the kitchen, the table has been laid.

CLARE Tea-time!

Polly and James run into the room.

POLLY Mum, can we take our tea in there? It's our serial.
JAMES Oh, please, Mum! It's brilliant. It's just going to start.

LOOKING FOR VICKY

CLARE Sit down. We don't eat in the sitting-room, you know perfectly well.

POLLY Oh, please! It's the last episode.

CLARE Where's Philippa?

JAMES She went to Susan's. She told me to tell you. Come on, Mum. Be nice for once.

CLARE When did she go?

JAMES Oh, I don't know. A few minutes ago. (*agony*) Oh, I can hear it starting.

TV-start-of-episode music can be heard as Clare goes to the front door, and looks out, looking for Philippa.

Polly and James pick up their plates of beans and fish fingers, and rush off.

POLLY Thanks, Mum.

Clare comes back, surveys the tea-table, laid for four, with bread, jams, a Swiss Roll, cheese, tomatoes, a plate of biscuits. She cuts herself a piece of cheese, and stands, staring out of the kitchen window, alone again.

Cut to a nearby heath.

A brackeny area with a few fir trees. Against one leans Red, owner of the motor bike, wearer of the heavy rings and dusty leather boots. He wears plastic sunglasses with pink frames, a leather jacket open to show his T-shirt with DISASTER AREA written on the front. His hair is short, and stands up in tufts. He smokes a cigarette thoughtfully.

Philippa, in her Vicky gear, steals up, throws a fir cone at him. He turns, comes to her, they embrace. He pushes her into some bracken, lies on top of her. We hear smothered giggles from Philippa, and see her hands tugging at his trousers.

End of Part One

Part Two

The heath. Six pm on a summer's evening. Philippa and Red are lying in the bracken. They sit up, Red stares into the distance. She giggles, and puts on his DISASTER AREA T-shirt.

PHILIPPA Hey, Red! Look. How d'you like me?

He looks at her, fondles her breasts absently and shrugs.

PHILIPPA Oh, come on! You're not very friendly today, are you? What's the matter?

Red rolls over on his stomach, away from her.

RED Andy's kicked me out, that's all. Lost me room. Got nowhere to kip down, have I?
PHILIPPA Andy's kicked you out? Why?
RED Don't ask me questions. I don't like it.
PHILIPPA Sorry.
RED I thought I might stay with you tonight. At your place.
PHILIPPA Mmmm! That'd be nice. A whole night! (*It's an act: she sighs*) But ...
RED (*testing her*) I thought ... why don't we go round there straight away? I fancy that, seeing your room, and all.
PHILIPPA You know about it. I've told you lots of times. I've got this landlady, and she doesn't let me have anyone in, let alone a bloke. Honestly, she'd go mad. I'm sorry.
RED OK, OK, it don't matter. I can sleep rough, right? I don't have to have anywhere.

She touches him.

PHILIPPA Oh, Red, I really am sorry.
RED (*shaking her off*) I didn't expect you to help, did I? Bloody hell!

He rolls over to face her, forcing her to lie back, pinioning her wrists on the ground above her head. He stares into her face.

RED Blackwood 235.
PHILIPPA What about it?
RED Your phone number, innit?
PHILIPPA (*wary*) That's right.
RED Bracken Tops.
PHILIPPA Yes?
RED Where you live?

PHILIPPA Yes.
RED Top-floor flat.
PHILIPPA Let go. You're hurting me. Why are you asking all these silly questions? You know where I live.
RED Right. Vicky le Fleming. Blackwood 235. Bracken Tops. Top-floor flat. (*He lets her go*) Just testing me memory, thasall. (*Scratches himself*) Got to keep myself up to scratch. I'm getting old. Don't want to start forgetting things.
PHILIPPA You certainly are in a funny mood today.
RED When Andy kicked me out, I got this idea about coming to your place. Social Security don't like it if you haven't got an address. (*pause*) So I phoned you up.
PHILIPPA (*freezes*) What?
RED Phoned you up.
PHILIPPA (*speaking fast, playing for time*) But I told you, I'm not allowed phone calls. You can only phone when I tell you, like the other day when she was out. (*Pause plucks up courage.*) What happened?
RED You weren't in, were you?
PHILIPPA So what happened?

Red looks away from her, calculating, then grins.

RED Nothing happened, did it? No answer. Phone rang and rang, but there was no bleeding answer.

Philippa is relieved. She laughs, and pulls him to her.

Later, in the kitchen, Clare and Derek are eating supper. The meal reflects a way of life limited by a large mortgage, an expensive season ticket, and three growing children: macaroni cheese with a green salad, and a can of beer each. They eat in silence.
Derek is in his office clothes, but with his tie off. He has a grey end-of-day look. He eats noisily, absorbed in his food, and is untidy with lettuce.
Clare watches him. Pushes her helping to one side.

CLARE Well? Aren't you going to say anything?
DEREK Sorry? What?
CLARE Look, you haven't got to *be* here. That's all right; I'm the one who has to cope with it all. But I just thought you could at least *say* something. Tell me what you think I ought to do about it. Help in some way.
DEREK I have. (*Mouth full*) I did, darling. I said . . . (*Swallows, and*

helps himself to more from the dish) I said . . . (*Shrugs*) it must have been very annoying for you. I do sympathise.

CLARE I spent the entire morning answering the telephone. I was scared. I even had to go out this afternoon, and walk round the bloody shops, just so that I wouldn't be here.

DEREK That's awful; that's really awful. (*A thought*) Mind you, it was silly of you to go out. Goodness knows when we'll get the phone connected now.

CLARE I told you. I left a note for the telephone men. They would have waited.

DEREK They never wait, you know. They've always got somewhere else to go to.

CLARE For God's sake, Derek! I was frightened!

Derek spoons up more macaroni.

DEREK Shall I finish this up, or would you like some?

CLARE What's the point of playing squash every lunch-time, if you're going to have three helpings of macaroni cheese at night?

Derek gets up, and looks in the fridge.

DEREK Is there another can of beer anywhere?

CLARE I think I must be going mad. Look, I must talk to you about these phone calls. How do I know he won't come here tomorrow? He said he was coming round.

DEREK I might take up jogging, I thought.

He has found a can of beer, and brings it to the table.

CLARE What if he's dangerous – you know, psychopathic? Derek, please, I know you think I'm being very boring.

DEREK (*opening his can*) No, darling. No.

CLARE Just tell me what you think. Please.

Derek thinks, drinks beer, shakes his head, laughs.

DEREK We have a few rum phone calls at the office. When was it? Last year. Sylvia took the calls to start with, but we all got involved in the end. Had a thing about underwear.

CLARE (*loses her temper*) Christ! You're so thick. It's this bloody house, can't you see? Oh, you thought it was such a good idea! Let's move to the country. Fresh air for the kids. Wide open spaces. Nice polite country schools. A big garden.

DEREK Big mortgage!
CLARE Yes, a big mortgage. And macaroni cheese and cans of beer for supper. Oh, yes! Well, you left one thing out of account in all that, didn't you?
DEREK Remember when we used to have wine every night, when we were first married?
CLARE I said, you left one thing out of account. You didn't think about me. Not once.
DEREK Of course I thought about you.
CLARE Oh, yes, I just love being cooped up in an empty house. It doesn't matter that I've no one to talk to, all day long. I've got plenty to do – the washing, and the ironing and the tidying and cleaning the lavatory, and of course all the driving – such fun! I'm having a great time; I love it, what with a herd of savage dogs next door, and maniacs on the telephone – it's a social whirl, I'm telling you. While you're slaving away at your office, I'm having a terrific time.
DEREK We discussed the whole thing. I wouldn't have moved out here without consulting you. You know that. We talked about it for months.
CLARE (*simple*) You said it was for the children. And I believed you.

Derek looks at her, picks the crust off the macaroni dish, eats it absently, gets up, yawns.

DEREK Come on. I'll help clear away, shall I? And then early to bed, I think, for both of us. I've got a ten o'clock meeting with P.G., so I want to be fresh in the morning.

He puts two plates on the draining board.

DEREK There! I'll just get my book, and go up. Don't be long, darling, will you?

Clare gets up, puts on her rubber gloves, and opens the dishwasher.

Next day, they are all in the car expect Derek, who is doing breathing exercises, and Philippa, who is late as usual. Clare sounds the horn.

JAMES She's *always* late.

Derek stops doing exercises, and says to Clare:

DEREK Look, I know. I'll phone Telecom myself the minute I get in, and really give them a rocket. Leave it to me. And (*lowers voice*) about the other thing, don't worry. I'm sure it was nothing.

CLARE I don't see how it could have been *nothing*.

DEREK Well, I don't mean nothing as such; I mean nothing important – nothing to worry about. (*Looks around*) Where is that bloody girl? (*To Clare*) Listen, if anything does happen, get to a phone. I mean, go next door –

CLARE Next *door*!

DEREK Well, or somewhere. Get to a phone, and ring me at once, OK? I'll get in touch the les gendarmes toute de suite. But I don't for one minute think –

POLLY Why is Dad talking in French?

CLARE Don't interrupt.

Philippa, in school uniform, looking very young and scrubbed, gets into the car.

DEREK There you are, madam! And about bloody time too! I'm going to miss my train, and get the sack, and then we'll all be bankrupt.

Out on the heath, Red in lying in a sleeping bag under a clump of bracken. He rolls to a sitting position, shivering, lights a cigarette with trembling fingers, and sits huddled in his bag, thinking. Then he looks at his watch, gets up, and rolls up his bag. Nearby is his motorbike.

Clare, returning, alone in the car, drives past the roadman, who waves.
The motorbike is now parked off the drive behind a bush. Red peers through a downstairs window.
At the sound of the car approaching, he runs off quickly into the bushes.
Clare gets out of her car. She is holding a loaf, twin toilet rolls, and a jumbo bottle of bleach. She runs into the house, slams the door, and turns the radio on. It is a phone-in.

VOICE It makes my blood boil.

As the phone-in continues Clare sips coffee, takes a bite of toast, then tips a basket of washing onto the floor to sort, chucking items into the washing-machine. Almost at once she comes across the

DISASTER AREA T-shirt. It puzzles her. She sniffs it, holds it up, then, looking around to make sure she is not observed, takes off her blouse, and tries it on. Meanwhile:

VOICE As a house-owner and a mother, I feel very strongly about it, I have to say.

INTERVIEWER Thank you, Brenda.

VOICE Can I make one more point, Dave? Have I got time?

INTERVIEWER Fire away, Brenda.

VOICE The thing that really annoys me, Dave, and it's my own personal experience, is – well, you take our local park, Westwood Park – I don't know if you've heard of it. Well, I take my little girl, Sharon – she's three – to play on the grass there every afternoon.

INTERVIEWER That's Sharon?

VOICE That's Sharon. I take her to the park every afternoon, and quite honestly, it's disgusting. They're absolutely everywhere. You have to be on your guard everywhere you look. I don't want to be vulgar on the radio, but you know to what I'm referring, don't you?

INTERVIEWER Yes, we all do, Brenda.

VOICE I mean, people take their dogs into the park to do their business, –

Clare goes into the hall to look at herself in the mirror. There is a loud knock on the door. She jumps, runs into the kitchen.

VOICE – and I take Sharon to the park to play on the grass.

Clare grabs her blouse, which she drapes over her shoulders.

VOICE It's a collision course.

INTERVIEWER It certainly is.

Clare switches the radio off then opens the door to find Red leaning against the lintel.

CLARE Are you the telephone man?

RED (*after a pause*) Yeah! I'm the telephone man; that's right. (*He grins*) The telephone man.

CLARE Ah! Good. Well, come in. This way. Is it just you?

RED (*following*) It's just me –

Clare indicates the phone, which is still disconnected.

CLARE Here it is. I don't suppose it'll take long will it?

Red picks up the phone thoughtfully.

CLARE There was something about not having enough cabling. Have you brought enough cabling today?
RED Hard to say.
CLARE Well, I certainly hope so. It's to go in the kitchen.

She leads him into the kitchen, and he sits down in her chair.

CLARE We thought, over here on the dresser.

She turns, and sees him. He picks up her coffee, and sips it, she is speechless.

RED I don't usually drink coffee.
CLARE Oh! Actually it was mine.
RED (*polite*) Is that a fact?

She looks at him. Something is wrong. She moves to the window, and looks out. Then back to him.

CLARE There's no van out there. Where's your van? Where are your tools?
RED Who the bleeding hell do you think I am?
CLARE You said you were the telephone man.
RED I thought you meant about yesterday – all that stuff.
CLARE What stuff?

Red speaks into the telephone he is holding, imitating her voice.

RED 'No. No. No one of that name 'ere. Certainly not. If you don't stop bothering me, I'm going to call the police.' (*Slams down the receiver*) What you done with it? Torn it off the wall or summing? You was afraid I might bother you again, and you tore it right out, didn't you?

He stands up. She is so scared that she can't speak. He takes his plastic sunglasses from a pocket of his leather jacket, and puts them on. A silence. Then . . .

CLARE What do you want?
RED Same as yesterday. I'm looking for Vicky.
CLARE There's no Vicky here. I told you.
RED And I told you I was coming over.
CLARE There's no Vicky here.
RED I don't believe you. I'll see for myself.

He moves slowly towards her. She clutches the blouse round her.

RED Why are you covering up your tits like that?

He rips back the blouse and see the DISASTER AREA T-shirt.

RED That's interesting.
CLARE Please go away.
RED When I'm ready. I slept rough last night. Out there, know what I mean? Not far away. In me sleeping-bag. Only trouble was, I couldn't hardly sleep a wink.

The camera becomes Clare, looking for a weapon. There's a kitchen knife on the draining board. Camera passes it, then comes back to it.

RED That was what I was phoning about yesterday. Got chucked out of me room. I wanted to ask Vicky if I could kip down in her room, but when I see her, she says No; her landlady wouldn't like it. Her landlady. (*He grips her wrist*) That's you. It was horrible out there – animals – could be anything, scuttling and rustling all the bleeding night long. I nearly came and knocked on the door. I was so spooked up. But I thought I'd better wait till morning. (*He looks at the table*) Goldilocks and the three bears – breakfast already on the table. I haven't had mine yet.

He releases her, and picks up a piece of toast.

RED You should have remembered the bowls of porridge.

She picks up the knife.

CLARE Please go away. This knife is very sharp. I'm not going to use it; I'm simply warning you. I don't know what you want; I don't know what you're after; I can't imagine why anyone should want to hang about me and my house like this. But whatever it is, forget it. Just get out! Out!

He watches her, leaning against the wall, smiling.

RED Knife, eh? I really like knife wounds. I got scars already? (*Pulls up sleeve to show her*) I did these myself, but you can have a go. I collect them. Come on, give us a good scar.
CLARE Get . . . Out.
RED She told me you was a nutter.
CLARE *Who* told you?

RED   (*spells it out*) Vicky told me. Told me you was a nutter.
CLARE   (*tries to laugh*) I can't stand this. Vicky doesn't exist. It's all in your head.
RED   I saw her last night, and I asked her, 'Who's that cow I keep getting when I phone you up?' And she says, 'My landlady. She's a nutter.' (*Pause*) So I'll just go up and find her, OK?
CLARE   If you go upstairs, I shall phone for the police.

He picks up the phone from the table.

RED   I'll dial 999 for you, shall I? Or would you like to do it?

He throws the phone to her, but she does not try to catch it.

RED   Whoops! Butterfingers!
CLARE   There's a phone next door. I can use it any time. It would take me two minutes to get there. I strongly advise you to leave.

Red shrugs, and moves out of the kitchen. Clare follows, still holding the knife.

CLARE   Please, I can hear the telephone men. I can hear the van. If you go now, I won't take the matter any further.

He goes to the foot of the stairs.

CLARE   There's nothing of value up there, if that's what you want.

He stops, turns, and looks at her.

RED   Why don't you run off, then, and make your phone call? It's only two minutes. Phone the police. You don't have to come up with me.
CLARE   This is my house. Those are my bedrooms. You can't just go –
RED   I'm beginning to think you and Vicky are in this together, hiding summing from me. What's the big mystery? Come on! I don't like people kidding me around.

He goes on up, and she follows.

RED   Vicky! Vicky! Where are you, you bitch?
CLARE   You're mad. There's no one here.

He opens a bedroom door and looks in.

RED   Look, I know she's somewhere. Apart from anything else, you've got my bleeding T-shirt on. Look! (*Picks a piece of bracken from Clare's chest*) See this? These bits of stick? That's where we lay down.

Clare stares at the T-shirt. Pause. An important moment. Suddenly she understands the whole thing.
She stares at Red. She is no longer afraid, but horrified.

RED What you looking at? What's the matter?
CLARE (*quietly*) Come in here.

She leads him into Philippa's bedroom. It is chaotically untidy. A homemade mobile of rock stars spins slowly round and round above the bed. A rocking horse wears a horror mask. A teddy bear sits facing the wall. A penknife is stuck into the wall. There are weird posters, objects trouves, candles. On a shelf by the window is a collection of carved wooden birds. Notice on the outside of the door read 'PRIVATE. PHILIPPA WATKINS. KEEP OUT'. There is a photo on the mantelpiece of Philippa in school uniform, holding a cup, and smiling.
Clare throws the picture to him.

CLARE Is this who you're looking for?
RED Jesus!
CLARE School uniform.
RED Right.
CLARE That is Vicky, I take it?
RED Right.

He turns it over.

RED This year?
CLARE Right.
RED Jesus!
CLARE Right. She's fourteen. But you'd know that, of course.

He stares at Clare, then walks to the door, and reads the notice.

RED This her room, is it?
CLARE That's right.
RED (*pointing to the photo*) *Her* room?
CLARE Right.

Red gives a low whistle of alarm. It is his turn to be frightened. He puts on his dark glasses, and moves onto the landing.
Clare quickly gets between Red and the top of the stairs. Now she is taking control.

CLARE Where do you think you're going?
RED I told you. I gotta find a place.
CLARE What about the famous Vicky? What's happened to her all of a sudden? (*Points to bedroom*) Get back in there.

He tries to push past her.

RED Sorry. I gotta get going.

Now she looks as if she really will use the knife.

CLARE I said 'Get back in there'. Don't imagine you can just walk off. Please.
RED Make your mind up. A minute ago, you was *telling* me to push off.

She drives him back into the room, using the knife, shuts the door behind her, and leans against it.

CLARE It's about time you explained things, don't you think?

Red tries to figure out how to get past her.

RED What?
CLARE You pester me on the telephone. You wangle your way into my house, pretending to be a telephone engineer. You claim to know my daughter, but under another name. I'd really quite like to know what's going on.

One hand behind her, she locks the door, and takes out the key, showing it to him.

RED What've you –
CLARE Sit down.

He sits on the bed. Makes an attempt to be casual. Picks up Philippa's diary, opens it, takes off his sunglasses to read it.

RED 'This diary belong to Ph . . .'?
CLARE Philippa.
RED 'Philippa Watkins'. (*Shuts diary with a snap*) Philippa! Shit!
CLARE And she's fourteen.

Red takes out a packet of cigarettes, and offers her one.

CLARE No. Thank you.

He lights up with a shaking hand. Stands up.

RED OK. It's me own fault. I walked right into it, didn't I? I knew she was up to something, and I thought I'd catch her out. And then, when I got you on the phone, it turned into quite a giggle. But I shouldn't have come round today; that was pushing it. Come on, give us the key.

CLARE How about telling me your name?
RED You've got no right, locking me in here.
CLARE Sit down!

Red sits on the bed again.

RED All right, all right. You don't have to shout.
CLARE How did you come to meet Philippa?
RED Just met her.
CLARE Where?
RED Around.
CLARE Where exactly?
RED Disco.
CLARE She's never been to a disco.
RED I met her at a disco.
CLARE Which disco?
RED Highwayman.
CLARE The Highwayman? That's the pub in Witherington. Well, I suppose they *could* have a disco. How long ago?
RED About a month.
CLARE And just how many times have you seen her since?
RED (*shrugs*) Forget.
CLARE How often?
RED I dunno.
CLARE Most evenings?
RED I dunno.
CLARE Out there on the heath? (*To herself*) That's it, of course. That's where she's been going. (*To Red*) And what did you do on the heath every night, with my daughter?
RED Nothing. I told you. I didn't do nothing. You ask Vicky.
CLARE Philippa. I will. But at the moment I'm asking you.

He walks agitatedly to the window.

RED Look, I know what you're on about. Ever since you locked the door, I've seen what you're driving at.
CLARE I don't know what you mean.
RED It's the under-age bit, isn't it? Mummy's innocent little girl, only fourteen and never been . . You're thinking of turning me over, aren't you?

CLARE (*shocked*) Are you telling me ...? Are you admitting ...?
RED I'm not telling you nothing about that. I'm just warning you, you see. You're not sticking that underage thing on me. You want to get to know your own daughter a bit better, you do.
CLARE What do you mean?
RED Ask her what she's been up to this last year or so.
CLARE What?
RED You ask her. Ask the little tart what she's been doing. Right? Before you start accusing other people.
CLARE I don't know what –
RED (*looking out of the window*) Oh, look! Real live genuine little telephone men coming down your drive.

Clare comes to the window, and looks.

CLARE Oh! ... Oh, I'll just ...

She moves towards the door. He follows.

CLARE You're not coming. You get back over there.
RED Open the bloody door. Come on.
CLARE I'm locking it after me. You needn't think I've finished with you yet.
RED Think I'm crazy? I'm not staying here.

Sound of knocking at the front door.

RED Come on! (*tries to wrest the key from her hand*) Come on, you silly cow!
CLARE Leave me alone!
RED Give me the key!

They struggle. The knife drops from Clare's hand. They are very close together. A moment. She realises how much she fancies him. Mutual recognition in both of what has been going on beneath the surface of the scene so far. Silence. Then:

RED I could stay if you like.

Quite a long pause, as the implications of this sink in.

CLARE No, I don't think so, thanks. I think you'd better go.

He moves away from her, back to the window, and looks down. Sound of knocking on the front door.

Outside Fred is at the door and Eric is peering through the kitchen window.

FRED I'll knock again. Typical, isn't it? Husband rings up, and gives a load of mouth. We turn up –

ERIC And his missus has gone out for the day.

In the bedroom, Red looks down through the window, then turns to her.

RED They're going away. There's only you and me. Nobody to know.

He moves back towards her.

CLARE (*shaken*) No, I really think not. I really couldn't . . . I'll just . . .

She unlocks the door, and opens it.

RED (*gentlemanly and polite*) I do fancy you, you know.

CLARE Yes. But it wouldn't do, I'm afraid, any more than . . . It really wouldn't do. Please go now.

Small pause.

RED Right.

He goes past her, out onto the landing, and down the stairs.
She goes over to the window, and watches Red walking away. He doesn't look back.
She flops on the bed, shuts her eyes, then hugs herself. She is smiling, enjoying what has happened.

CLARE Wow!

She starts to laugh, opens her eyes, sees Red's sunglasses on the bedside table, picks them up, and puts them on the teddy bear. She sits on the bed again, lies back, closes her eyes and relaxes.

Later in the day, Clare and Derek are standing, looking at the garden. She has put a shirt or blouse on over the DISASTER AREA T-shirt but is still wearing it, though it can't be seen. He takes off his tie.

DEREK A whole two hours early! What luxury (*breathes the air*) Ah! You've no idea what this means to me. Just to breathe the air. When I get out of the car in the evenings. I want to kiss the earth. I could get down on my knees and kiss it.

Clare smiles.

DEREK You've no idea what it's like in my office with the new air-conditioning. My sinuses start up the minute I get in. You can hardly breathe. The only thing that makes it bearable is having this to come home to. I look out of my window – traffic fumes, people dashing and scurrying about like ants, and I shut my eyes and think of the garden, and you in a deck chair. Life of Riley – that's what my old man would have said. She's got the life of Riley.

They start to walk indoors.

CLARE The life of Riley!

The kitchen is still a mess, with the clutter of breakfast uncleared, washing still on the floor, and the telephone where Red threw it. Derek is dismayed.

DEREK What the .... You haven't done breakfast. Why on earth ...? What's happened? Why haven't you cleaned up?
CLARE I'm not quite sure really.
DEREK You're not *sure*! And the phone!

He picks it up. Its wires trail in the air.

DEREK It's not connected.
CLARE I know.
DEREK You said they'd been.
CLARE I didn't.
DEREK (*shouts*) You did! In the car. You distinctly told me they'd been.

Philippa comes in, and Derek moderates his tone with difficulty.

DEREK In the car, I said to you, 'Did the men come?' and you said, 'Yes'.

Philippa takes a banana and sighs.

CLARE Well, I must have meant to say, 'No'. I couldn't have said 'Yes' because they didn't come. You can see that.

Philippa is buttering a slice of bread.

PHILIPPA Um . . . Excuse me. I'm going round to Susan's in a few minutes. OK?

Clare looks at her sharply.

CLARE Oh, all right, dear. Don't be too late back.
PHILIPPA I won't.

She goes out, with her bread and banana.

DEREK So they *didn't* come?
CLARE No.
DEREK I shall have to go straight out again – having only just got back – and find a telephone. (*Looks at his watch*) Five o'clock! I might still catch them. My God, I'm going to give them such a rocket. And while I'm gone, for Christ's sake, let's get organised shall we? If you weren't out, what did you do all day?
CLARE I went to sleep.
DEREK All day long?
CLARE No. Not all day long.
DEREK It's not much to ask. You've got a dishwasher and a washing-machine. All you have to do is press a few knobs.
CLARE If it's just pressing a few knobs, then there's really no need to fuss, dear. It won't take a minute.

She turns her back on him, and begins clearing up.
Derek hesitates, then goes out. Clare listens for the departing car. After a pause she takes off her top, revealing the DISASTER AREA T-shirt.

Later. Out on the heath, Philippa is in her Vicky gear. She clumsily lights a cigarette and takes a big drag at it. She's waiting for Red, ready to look casual the moment he appears. In another part of the heath, Clare, in the DISASTER AREA T-shirt, is looking for Philippa.

Meanwhile in the kitchen Polly is playing her recorder. Derek comes in from the hall.

DEREK No luck. I'll have to phone again in the morning. Where's Mummy?
POLLY Popped out.
DEREK Popped out?
POLLY Gone for a walk, she said.

Angrily Derek begins to load the dishwasher. Polly plays on. The recorder again.

Out on the heath Philippa sees in the distance a DISASTER AREA T-shirt approaching. She thinks it is Red. She leans back against the tree, looks the other way, and puts on a bored look, though she can't help a small gleam of excitement. She arranges her jacket so that her breasts can be seen. She is ready to receive him. Hearing footsteps she tenses slightly. Then turns her head, wearing her carefully arranged expression – a little bored, a little pouting, a little enticing; it's the expression she always has on these occasions. The expression changes as she sees who is approaching. Clare looks at her, giving nothing away.

Cut back to the heath. Philippa starts to cry: she can't cope. Clare goes to her, and takes her in her arms, strokes her hair. A moment of understanding and reconciliation.

Finally we pull back to them as two small figures on a landscape, and we hear bird song, the cuckoo, and the gentle rustle of leaves. The same rustic idyll with which we began.

A Night of the Campaign

by Robin Glendinning and Leonard Kingston

An Introduction by Robin Glendinning

I always wanted to write, but every time I sat down in front of a blank sheet of paper I couldn't think of anything to write about. I tried short stories and poems, mainly on the grounds that they were short, but I always gave up. I made rules about setting aside an hour of every day or writing five thousand words a week but no sooner had I made these rules than I abandoned them.

Then in 1969 the society in which I lived began to fall apart in the most spectacular fashion. For years I had been vaguely aware that the political system of Northern Ireland was unhealthy: it seemed wrong that one's political views should be predetermined by one's religion. Catholics were nationalist and Protestants, like me, were unionist, and the unionist majority discriminated against the nationalist minority in various ways. I was too busy getting on with my own life to bother too much with all of this. I had been teaching History and English and had just got married and set up house. I was heavily involved with school drama, I fished, kept bees and played cricket, golf and rugby. The idea that I should take a personal stand on the shortcomings of the political system in my native province never entered my head. But now the place was going up in flames.

My wife Lorna and I joined an organisation called the 'New Ulster Movement' which was dedicated to promoting moderate reformist politics in a society that was becoming increasingly and dangerously polarised. Out of this movement was born the Alliance Party of Northern Ireland, which aimed at ending strife by combining both Catholic and Protestant in one political party. We were founder members.

Creating a new political party was very exciting. We met and talked to people of all sorts of views. We canvassed door to door to get new members all over

Northern Ireland. Party meetings often produced a vigorous clash of ideas: Nurturing non-sectarian politics was not easy when violent events provoked a very different reaction from each side of the community. We had to find a new way of speaking, a new language, to express the moderate, centre point of view. At last Catholic and Protestant Ulster people were actually talking frankly to each other. It was exhilarating. I addressed meetings, wrote speeches, reports, policy documents and made press releases. I also began to write stories and plays, and to get them broadcast on radio.

Politically I was not so successful. Although the party gained seats in both the Northern Ireland Assembly and in its successor The Convention I personally lost two deposits as a candidate. Instead of entering parliament I became the party's full time organizer and moved to Belfast. After three years I went back to teaching in a school in the centre of the city. The political life was too disorganised and I now wanted to concentrate on writing. I was still in touch with local events as many of them seemed to happen outside the front gates of the school.

My first stage play, called *Stuffing It*, was presented at the Dublin theatre festival and a television producer, Andree Molyneux saw it and commissioned me to write a forty minute television piece for a series of new writers. I sold her the idea of a play based on my canvassing experiences.

When I sat down to write the play I chose a sixteen year old school girl as my heroine because I wanted to capture that näive enthusiasm we had all felt at the beginning of the Alliance Party and to set it against the world-weary cynicism that came later from bitter experience. In a way the play is about loss of innocence. It is about a teenager coming to terms with the reality of the adult world, of discovering that things are never quite what they appear to be. It is also about how stupid the adults can be and how they can lose sight of the true goal while practising the complicated rules of the game. It may seem a rather bizarre adult world that Susan confronts but it is not all that strange: terrorism, conflict, injustice, ignorance, extremism and poverty seem all too normal in the world to-day.

All this was my ideal, but if it has been realised I owe

it to my co-writer Leanord Kingston. Although I did several initial re-writes the project had collapsed when he gave me a phone call. Would I mind if he 'played about with it a bit'? He thought it had 'potential'. I said that I would be delighted. Later that summer he sent me a much longer version. He had taken each of my scenes and characters and pushed them much further, developed the conflict and the drama. I re-wrote what he had written and then he re-wrote what I had done. And thus we became co-writers of the play that was eventually broadcast as a full length tele-drama in August 1985.

Most of the critics who liked it expressed surprise that we had been able to make comedy out of such apparently serious material. I was attacked from within the Alliance Party for having made fun of good people who were doing their utmost to 'save Northern Ireland from a bloody civil war'. I was upset by this because I thought I had written of all the characters with affection (with the exception of the know-all, drunk University lecturer). Even Margaret, it seemed to me, had something to be said for her. She was there, on the street, knocking on doors. She had a right to say what she thought and she was not afraid to say it. Too many people sit back and do and say nothing. She may have gone back to her middle class home with her views 'moderated'. At least she was giving them a chance. Sean needed to be aware of a world outside the ghetto. Alan's statement was a triumph of political compromise.

The play was billed as a comedy and of course I had set out to write a comedy. Looking at it now I find it sad. Perhaps I always thought it was sad. I still think it is true.

Robin Glendinning, 1987

The Cast

Susan Watson
Alan Smith
Mrs Watson
Mr Watson
Margaret Levy
Dermot Kane
Sean
Mrs Doherty
Joe Doherty
Bridie
O'Neill
Louis O'Neill
Mrs McMahon
Youth 1
Youth 2
Philip Pelham
Muriel Pelham
Newsreader
Loudspeaker

A Night of the Campaign

1 Outside School

Alan Smith, a gawky twenty-two year old trainee-teacher with briefcase and books, is hurrying out of school. A crowd of homeward-bound schoolgirls are pouring down the steps. At the bottom of the steps, with an eye on the approaching Alan, is Susan. They collide, and a book is sent scattering to the ground.

SUSAN   Oh, sorry, Mr Smith – didn't see you.
ALAN   Oh, Susan . . .

Both groping for the book, they collide again.

SUSAN   (*laughing*) Where are you rushing off to tonight, sir?
ALAN   (*embarrassed, and reaching for book which she is holding*) Oh, I've a few things to do . . .

Pretending to do so unconsciously, she holds the book just out of his reach.

SUSAN   You looking for any helpers?
ALAN   What for?
SUSAN   The Election . . . (*she whispers conspiratorially*) For the party.
ALAN   (*alarmed*) Who told you about that?
SUSAN   . . . Well, do you?
ALAN   (*about to go*) Ah, no . . . we've got enough help, thanks.
SUSAN   I'm not doing anything tonight.
ALAN   Thanks anyway – see you tomorrow. Bye bye.

He hurries off. Susan pulls an angry, rebellious face behind his back.

SUSAN   (*to herself*) That's what you think.

2 The Watson's Drawing Room

Mr Watson is deep in the local paper and Mrs Watson is looking at holiday brochures.

The television is on.
Susan sits on a sofa behind them, her exercise book open on her knee, but her eye is on the clock.
After a few minutes silence, she gets up.

SUSAN Well, it's time I went.
MRS WATSON Went? Went where?
SUSAN Oh. Out. Canvassing.
MRS WATSON You what? I do wish you'd speak up, Susan. Don't mumble.
SUSAN (*calm*) I wasn't mumbling. I said I'm going canvassing.
MRS WATSON What *is* she talking about, Des? Canvassing.
SUSAN For the bye-election.

Mrs Watson looks blank.

SUSAN I did explain, Mummy. I told you yesterday.
MRS WATSON You never said a word. Des, do you hear this?
WATSON What?
MRS WATSON Susan says she's going *canvassing*.
WATSON What?
SUSAN The bye-election, Dad. In West Belfast.
WATSON West Belfast? What about her homework?
MRS WATSON Yes, Susan. *Homework*.
SUSAN It's done. Don't worry.
WATSON But I do worry, I'm afraid.
SUSAN Then *don't*. Because I've done it.
WATSON All right, all right, none of your smart talk, miss. (*To his wife again*) *Where* is she going?
MRS WATSON (*shouting*) The bye-election!
SUSAN I'm an Alliance Party member. I have to support my party.
MRS WATSON Oh, Susan, really! You know perfectly well you only joined the Aly –
SUSAN (*sighing*) Al-liance. God, Mummy, don't you know anything about politics?
MRS WATSON Oh, Alliance! Well, I know enough about you, young lady, to know that it was just an excuse to go to their Young Disco with that student teacher.
WATSON Politics?

They both ignore him.

SUSAN I didn't.

MRS WATSON It wasn't? Little fibber!
SUSAN I've extended my interest, that's all.
MRS WATSON Oh? Oh? And where did you find the time for that?
SUSAN Oh, for God's sake, Dad! Do I have to eat, sleep and drink nothing but school work?
WATSON Yes! If you have the good fortune to go to a first class school, young lady. That is precisely what you should be doing. Now if you are to realise your potential . . .
MRS WATSON Oh, *do* shut up, Des! Go back to your reading – Susan, this is all that student teacher's fault!

Mr Watson snorts, and goes back into his paper.

SUSAN It's nothing to do with him!
MRS WATSON And West Belfast of all places –
SUSAN Well, unfortunately, Mummy, there doesn't happen to be a bye-election in South Belfast at the moment.
MRS WATSON No need for sarcasm!
SUSAN That was irony, Mummy.
MRS WATSON Oh, Des! Attend to your daughter, for Heaven's sake!
WATSON (*irritated*) Eh? – Well, just tell her! She's not going!
MRS WATSON I've already told her!
WATSON *Homework!*
SUSAN I've done my homework!
WATSON Study then! Study! –
SUSAN How the hell can –
WATSON Or watch the telly! – (*with a triumphant laugh at his wife*) Panorama! There! That's politics.

Susan glares angrily at them both.

SUSAN Yes, that's about your level, isn't it? Watch the tele. Shut your eyes to the real world – I'm ashamed for both of you, do you know that? You – you want me to be like all the rest at school. All exams and UCCA forms! And running off to – to University in England – we've got to get out there! Direct political action! That's what is needed. Are you listening to me?
MRS WATSON Yes, pet, yes pet.
SUSAN If you're not part of the solution then you're part of the problem! And, Christ, are you two some problem!
MRS WATSON Oh! What a thing to say!
WATSON Direct political – Christ – what sort of language is that?

Susan makes for the door.

MRS WATSON (*jumping up*) Don't just sit there! Stop her!
WATSON (*not stirring*) Come back.
SUSAN (*turning in the doorway*) I'm sixteen! I'm not an infant. I refuse to be turned into a – a political eunuch, just to please your medieval minds!

She exits proudly, slamming the front door behind her.

WATSON (*after a long, stunned silence*) Has she gone upstairs?
MRS WATSON No! That was the front door.

Silence.

WATSON Whatever next.

Silence.

MRS WATSON She can't be allowed to carry on like this.

They both sigh, and sink back into their seats.

MRS WATSON Very naughty.
WATSON (*already reading again*) I shall speak to her.

3 South Belfast Alliance Headquarters

A long trestle table, with folding chairs. On it is a large typewriter, campaign literature, leaflets, etc, a telephone near one end and a radio at the other.
There is a wall map of Belfast, showing electorial boundaries, and various posters. 'End the Nightmare – Vote Alliance', says one. 'Alliance unites people', says another.
Alan Smith, offering clipboards with parts of the electorial register attached to Margaret Levy, a handsome fierce-eyed lady of forty, and Dermot Kane, a slight, dreamy, occasional stutterer about the same age.

ALAN Kashmir?
MARGARET (*unenthusiastically*) Mmn.

She passes the board on to Dermot.
Susan creeps into the room, her coat on over her school uniform.

SUSAN (*grinning*) Alan!

Alan looks up in surprise and alarm, and gives a frozen half smile.

He looks down again, flustered, and gropes among the clipboards.

ALAN   Er, Margaret, this is . . .
SUSAN   Susan. Hi, I'm here to help.
ALAN   Where was I?
MARGARET   Calcutta Street.
ALAN   Sorry, Margaret. Yes. Ah. Bombay. (*Susan sits down beside him*) And . . . er . . . Cawnpore.
SUSAN   (*whispering urgently*) Alan –
ALAN   (*loudly*) Cawnpore!
MARGARET   (*exasperated*) Where is the regular ward organiser?
ALAN   Ward – I think this is his evening for his, well, driving lesson. (*lamely*) I think.
MARGARET   I thought at least the agent would be here.
ALAN   I'm not sure where he is.
MARGARET   I see.
ALAN   Don't worry Margaret. Everything's under control. I've all the literature.

Reaching across, his hand meets Susan's straying amongst the leaflets. He pushes them aside.

ALAN   Complaints, housing, street lighting, pavement, harrassment.
MARGARET   (*sharply*) What?
ALAN   (*confused*) Sorry?
MARGARET   You said 'harrassment'.
ALAN   You know – by the Brits.
MARGARET   'Brits'?
ALAN   Yes. It crops up. Sometimes.
MARGARET   It makes me thoroughly sick, the sneering way people refer to them as 'Brits'. As if they were some species of Stone Age Man.
ALAN   The British Army, I –
MARGARET   *The* Army, young man. There is only one army. *Our* army.

Dermot giggles nervously. Margaret turns on him.

MARGARET   Dermot. Whether we are Protestant *or* Catholic. Our army.
ALAN   Well, should there be any . . . complaints.
MARGARET   Yes. Nothing obviously – silly of me to ask – on how we might investigate *Army* complaints re harrassment by the local population.

ALAN (*laughing apologetically*) Well ... soldiers don't have a vote in this election.

MARGARET The one who died this morning certainly didn't. Let's not forget that. A young life senselessly blasted away.

SUSAN (*a gleam in her eye*) There was another young life blasted away yesterday. In Divis.

ALAN (*trying to steer the conversation away from danger*) Education?

SUSAN A local girl.

ALAN Future policy! Health and Social Services.

He thrusts more leaflets at Margaret.

MARGARET Well, take them Dermot.

Dermot take them, sneaking a sly grin at Susan.

MARGARET Now. Will my car be safe?

ALAN Oh, well, immobilise it. Have you a Krooklock?

MARGARET No.

ALAN Ah, well, take out the rotor arm.

MARGARET Do you know –

Dermot is still grinning at Susan.

MARGARET Dermot, wake up! Do you know what a rotor arm is?

DERMOT Rotor arm?

MARGARET Can you take it out?

SUSAN Oh, that's simple.

A look from Alan checks her.

DERMOT Yes. Anything you say, Margaret.

MARGARET Come on then.

DERMOT Right!

ALAN Oh, and Margaret! We're to meet up again at Sean's ...

MARGARET Springfield Gardens, Falls Road.

ALAN Yes, I've already –

MARGARET Already told us, yes ... Dermot!

She sweeps out.

ALAN Oh! And Cawnpore ...

But they have gone. He lets out a groan of exasperation.

SUSAN She's a real bitch, isn't she?

She rises, coming towards him.

ALAN What are you here for? Sticking your nose in.
SUSAN You're looking nice.
ALAN Looking nice?
SUSAN Well, you've got a new tie.
ALAN What are you talking about?
SUSAN It's the wrong colour, though. It clashes.
ALAN (*amazed*) Look, will you just shut up. Me and my clothes are a non-subject. (*waving his clipboard*) I have to do Cawnpore now. You realise? Just because of you.
SUSAN Don't worry. I'll do it.
ALAN You will not.
SUSAN I've come here to canvass.
ALAN Oh, my God.
SUSAN What's wrong?
ALAN I'm taking you home.
SUSAN Oh, lay off.
ALAN I'm going to put you in the car and take you home.
SUSAN You can't turn me away. I'm a party member.
ALAN Junior party member. Too young to go canvassing.
SUSAN Oh? And where does it say that in the party constitution?
ALAN You – You are not, *not* canvassing in West Belfast. Right?
SUSAN Why not?
ALAN Because it's dangerous – you'd stick out like a sore thumb – you'd probably end up raped.
SUSAN Oh, how infantile can you get.
ALAN (*panicking*) You are going home.
SUSAN Yes? How much do you bet?

4 Alan's Car

Alan is gloomily driving a battered Escort estate; Susan is sitting triumphantly beside him, and looking wide-eyed at the big slogans painted on high buildings – IRELAND UNFREE – SHALL NEVER BE AT PEACE.

SUSAN Jesus, how do they get up there to paint all that?
ALAN (*sneering*) They wear stilts.
SUSAN Oh, funny. Well, where are these Provies then?
ALAN (*wearily mimicking her*) Where are these Provies?
SUSAN That's what they call them, don't they? Well, where are they?

ALAN (*pointing sarcastically at a little old woman*) There! There they are! There's a Provie!
SUSAN Where? Her?
ALAN Yes, can't you see those trousers rolled up underneath her skirt?

Susan kneels up in her seat to look, forcing Alan to swerve.

ALAN For Christ's sake! Do you want us off the road!? Just sit still.

Susan sees another sign, NO TO COLLABORATORS, TOUTS AND QUIZLINGS.

SUSAN What are touts?

Alan refuses to reply.

5 Parking in Springfield Gardens

Alan fits an elaborate lock on the steering wheel.

SUSAN (*giggling*) Valuable antique, is it, sir?
ALAN A Ford is very easy to steal.
SUSAN (*looking around the deserted street*) Can't see any stealers around here.
ALAN No? Leave this unlocked for fiteen minutes, you won't see any car either.
SUSAN (*getting out*) Provies?
ALAN (*sarcastically*) No, no, mice.

Alan rings twice and Sean opens the door.
Sean, a lean twenty-eight year old appears in the darkened hall.

SEAN You've taken your time.
ALAN (*grimly indicating Susan*) Oh, local difficulties.
SEAN (*eyeing her uniform and grinning*) I'd call it a local opportunity. I like the outfit.
SUSAN Oh, you can borrow it if you like.
ALAN I'd be be careful how you insult this lady, Sean. She retaliates.

6 Sean's Room

It is bare and cheerless. A kitchen table piled with scattered campaign material and posters of Irish and Dublin pop groups on the walls.

SUSAN (*looking at the posters*) Is Sean a musician?

Alan is laying out his leaflets, and discovers a pile of Sean's leaflets. He frowns.

ALAN No, Sean is not a musician. He's a filthy pig. Stop that. (*She's looking in a drawer.*)
SUSAN I was only looking.
ALAN It's the looking I'm objecting to.
SUSAN When are we going to do that canvassing?
ALAN Sit down and be quiet.
SUSAN When are you going to stop sulking?
ALAN I am not sulking.
SUSAN (*to Sean*) He can't hold an intelligent conversation.
ALAN *I* . . .? I tell you, Sean, this wee girl –

Sean grins at Susan.

ALAN I have to teach her. Eight periods a week. She argues every point you make. You can't get a word in edgeways . . .
SUSAN Just 'cos he can't control the class.
ALAN Who could, with *you* in it! I promise you, once my teaching practice is up I'll be out of your snob school and back to Queen's like – that! (*trying unsuccessfully to click his fingers*)
SUSAN Like this?

Susan coolly clicks her fingers splendidly. Sean laughs.

ALAN Anyway, what about this Sean? These leaflets . . .
SEAN Ach! . . . Now he's onto me!
ALAN They're last year's stuff. Where's the new ones?
SEAN Where do you think, under the bed. What's it matter, nobody reads them anyway.
ALAN That's not the point, this stuff should be cleared out. And where are your canvassers then? You said you would get four or five.
SUSAN I'm one.
ALAN Susan, shut –

Susan pulls a face but subsides.

SEAN They're none too keen at the moment.
ALAN Why not?
SEAN It's been pretty lively around here, that kid being killed.

You try selling 'Alliance' amongst that. And we had a couple of kneecappings the other night.

ALAN What's that to do with it?

SUSAN (*eagerly*) Kneecappings?

SEAN The Provies said they knocked off an off-licence.

SUSAN Did they?

SEAN They were both drunk.

SUSAN And they were kneecapped for that. Jesus, they should come to our school disco.

SEAN Oh, the Provies are very moral.

SUSAN Are they?

SEAN (*solemn*) Only use French letters for priming bombs . . .

SUSAN Honest?

SEAN Have to get special dispensation even to handle the filthy Protestant things.

SUSAN (*laughs*) But for *bombs* . . .

SEAN Acid eats through the rubber and . . . wham! Well, it all amounts to the same thing in the end, doesn't it? Population control. Why, what do we Protestant schoolgirls use them for?

ALAN Sean, stop filling her with fairy tales. French letters are old hat –

SEAN Yes, it's Dutch caps . . .

ALAN It's mercury tilt now . . . What are we talking about bombs for? We've got to get started!

SUSAN Yes, let's start. I'm a canvasser. (*She reads from a leaflet*) 'Tick the positives, T for transport.'

Alan is trying, ineffectively, to snatch the leaflets away.

SUSAN I can manage all this. Easy. 'Billy Blyberg is the only candidate campaigning on both sides of the Peace Line!' There! I'll be sensational! Let me at them! I can win you votes, Alan, I bet you!

Alan groans, defeated. Sean grins.

7 Springfield Gardens

Sean, Susan and Alan come out to canvass.

SUSAN Blyberg for Belfast – *End* the *nightmare*! End the *nightmare*! Blyberg for Belfast – End –

SEAN Save it for the punters. Come on, Glenda Jackson . . .

ALAN Remember – Bill Blyberg got the lights turned on and the sewers fixed. Push that.

SEAN Right. Blyberg for shite and light.

They split off in different directions.

8 On the Streets

Walking through the door in the dividing wall, Sean points Susan into a small turning. Susan is slightly nervous now the moment for action has come. She looks up at the Republican posters in a window, hesitates, and moves on nervously past several other houses with posters. Seeing with relief a poster-free house, she knocks. A young woman opens the door. In the background there is the sound of cowboy film on television.

MRS DOHERTY Yes.

SUSAN (*consulting register*) Mrs Doherty?

MRS DOHERTY (*hesitant now*) Yes?

SUSAN I'm canvassing for Mr Blyberg.

Mrs Doherty looks blank.

SUSAN The bye-election.

MRS DOHERTY Oh. The election.

SUSAN Yes. Have you, er –

MRS DOHERTY (*shouting back into the house*) *Joe!*

JOE (*from inside*) What?

MRS DOHERTY Somebody canvassing! Joe!

Outburst of cowboy gunfire from television. No reply from Joe.

MRS DOHERTY *Somebody canvassing, Joe! For –* (*Looks at Susan*)

SUSAN Mr Blyberg.

MRS DOHERTY Mr Blyberg.

Increased volume of gunfire.

SUSAN The Alliance candidate.

MRS DOHERTY *The Alliance candidate Joe.*

SUSAN (*timidly*) It doesn't matter.

MRS DOHERTY *Joe!*

SUSAN Honestly, it doesn't matter.

MRS DOHERTY Ach, the big shite lies there watching television all night. (*Screaming*) Joeeeeee!

A door slams, and Joe appears. He is young, with beer belly and a scowl.

JOE What the hell is it?
MRS DOHERTY Young lady canvassing, Joe. Alliance.

Joe and Mrs Doherty turn their attention to Susan, who falls uneasily silent.

JOE Go on then.
SUSAN I'm canvassing for Bill Blyberg.
JOE Where is he?
SUSAN Mr Blyberg?
JOE Yeh.
SUSAN I don't know.
JOE You don't know?
SUSAN Canvassing somewhere else.
JOE They're always somewhere else. Go on.
SUSAN What?
JOE You've got more to tell us, haven't you? I'm listening. Maire's listening. Aren't you, Maire?
MRS DOHERTY Yes.
SUSAN Er ... Mr Blyberg ... (*With a discreet glance at her notes*) ... Is the only candidate canvassing on both sides of *The Peace Line*.
JOE Fascinating. Go on.
SUSAN Well ... er, he is the ... one person ... canvassing on both sides.
JOE Said that already.
SUSAN Well.

Stumped, she begins reading hurriedly.

SUSAN The Alliance party was founded in 1970.

Joe sniggers.

SUSAN We believe only the people of Northern Ireland can solve the problems of Northern Ireland. It unites Catholic and Protestant.
JOE In golf clubs.
SUSAN Golf clubs?
JOE It unites the middle classes.
SUSAN Oh. Well no! Not just the middle.....

In despair, she timidly proffers the leaflets.

A NIGHT OF THE CAMPAIGN

MRS DOHERTY (*taking pity on her*) Here, I'll take one.
JOE Answer me this.
SUSAN Yes?
JOE Why is there a foreign army in those streets out there?
SUSAN T-to keep the peace?
JOE Oh? And does it keep the peace?
SUSAN Well . . . I . . . yes. I suppose so. Some people think so.
JOE Oh, and I can guess who. You would know, wouldn't you. Where you from?
SUSAN None of your business.
JOE You're on my doorstep minding *my* business. You know where I live, now you tell me where *you* live.
MRS DOHERTY Joe . . .
SUSAN Stranmillis.
JOE Many soldiers round there?
SUSAN Not many.
JOE You won't notice if they went away then, would yer? It'll make bugger all difference to you. *You're* not going to get a plastic bullet in your kisser on the way to school in the morning.
MRS DOHERTY Joe, take it easy, she's only a girl.
JOE That's the point, isn't it? Condescending wee bitch!
MRS DOHERTY Joe!
JOE Well, where the hell is frigging Bill Blyberg? Is he afraid to come here that he has to send wee girls to canvas for him?
SUSAN I volunteered!
JOE (*quietly*) Oh, you volunteered, did you? Then perhaps you'd volunteer to take this back to Bill bloody Blyberg – (*Shoving a leaflet into her breast pocket*) – and tell him to stick it up his arse.

He turns and stomps back inside.

MRS DOHERTY He'll never vote for a Protestant.
SUSAN Why?
MRS DOHERTY Because he married one. And that's as far as he's going to go.

As Susan walks on, a Sinn Fein electioneering cavalcade passes by.

LOUDSPEAKER Vote Sinn Fein! Vote for the Party who stood behind the hunger strikers! Vote for the Party who has worked for you through our Advice Centres and full-time constituency service!

A vote for Sinn Fein is a vote against the British war machine that commits murder on our streets with plastic and with lead bullets!

A vote for Sinn Fein is a vote against administration of so-called British justice with its special powers, its strip searches, its show trials and its hired assassins, the RUC and the UDR!

Don't be misled by quislings and collatorators – vote SINN FEIN!! 'Ireland Unfree Shall Never Be At Peace!'

Susan retreats, bumping into a woman who has come to her doorstep to watch.

SUSAN   Oh – excuse me –
BRIDIE Nothing to excuse, dear. All my fault. Come in. We can't stand on the doorstep, can we.

She ushers Susan into her cosy living room.

SUSAN   I'm canvassing on behalf of –
BRIDIE It doesn't matter, dear. Don't catch your foot on that rug. Now – there we are – comfy, isn't it?

She settles into the armchair, motioning Susan to sit opposite.

SUSAN   I – I don't want to disturb you.
BRIDIE You're not disturbing me, dear.
SUSAN   But . . . I'm only canvassing . . .
BRIDIE And why wouldn't you be dear? Nothing wrong in that. Go on then. You tell me.

An open shoebox is on the floor. Susan looks inside and finds a tortoise.

BRIDIE Don't mind him.
SUSAN   No . . .
BRIDIE He's forty-two, dear. You wouldn't think it, would you?

She points to another unexpectedly close to Susan.

BRIDIE And this one – he's over fifty.
SUSAN   (*startled, moving away instinctively*) Oh . . . gosh.
BRIDIE (*laughs*) Course, I say, 'him' but, tell the truth, I don't know if they're boys or girls, really. You never catch them doing much – so you can't really tell. I expect that's why

they're such long livers. Can live to be a hundred and fifty, you know.

SUSAN Do they? Gosh . . .

Finally sitting gingerly, half expecting to find a tortoise in the armchair.

BRIDIE But why wouldn't they, dear? Sleep half the year. Peaceful. No chance to wear out.

SUSAN Yes. Very. Interesting. Er, this bye-election.

BRIDIE Oh! I forgot. Yes.

SUSAN I'm campaigning on behalf of Billy Blyberg, the Alliance candidate –

BRIDIE Good!

SUSAN Yes. Bill Blyberg is the only candidate campaigning on both sides of the Peace Line.

BRIDIE Ah . . .!

SUSAN Yes, he speaks for both sides. He's the only one who does.

BRIDIE (*nodding, impressed*) And he'd bring peace, would he, dear?

SUSAN Yes. Well . . . Yes.

BRIDIE Good. That's what we could do with. And will he bring back the buses? It's awful not having any buses in the evenings around here.

SUSAN (*doubtful now*) Oh yes . . .

BRIDIE Oh, and you get him to stop those youngsters putting things through the door!

SUSAN W-what things?

BRIDIE Ach, you know. Nasty things. They ought to be stopped.

SUSAN Oh.

BRIDIE Why only last week they were hammering on the door – you know, the way youngsters do. I went out and told a soldier. That was my big mistake, see. Never talk to a soldier, dear. Anyway, back they came and – oh. (*Laughs*) Well, would have been nothing, of course, except one of the tortoises walked in it. Spread it all over the carpet. Still it's all over now. But I think you ought to tell him.

SUSAN (*faint*) Yes. I'm really sorry.

BRIDIE What do you do, dear? What do you work at?

SUSAN Me? Oh, I'm still at school.

BRIDIE (*eager*) Ah! And what do you learn?

SUSAN Well, Maths, languages, French – German –

BRIDIE (*delighted*) Say something in French dear.

SUSAN Well . . .

INTENSIVE CARE

Bridie waits open-mouthed.

SUSAN Je suis une femme politique. I am a political lady. I think.
BRIDIE Oh very, very good. Here, Susan.

Searching in the cushions of her chair, she comes up with a small tortoise, and holds it out to her.

BRIDIE It's about your age.
SUSAN (*half-appalled, half-tempted*) Oh no . . . I couldn't.
BRIDIE But I *want* you to have it, dear. Here's a box. They're easy fed. And very clean – no messes, well, none to speak of. There, it'll be as happy as Larry in there.

Puts the tortoise in the box and hands it to Susan.

BRIDIE Now say something in German dear.
SUSAN Oh, yes. (*Holding up the shoebox*) Rict vielen Dank Fur Das . . . I'm afraid I don't know the word of tortoise –
BRIDIE Oh.
SUSAN Ah! I know the word for *thingummy* in German – Dingsbum. (*triumphantly*) Dank Fur Das Dingsbum!
BRIDIE Dingsbum! Oh, what a lovely name!

Both laughing, they chant the sentence together.

9 In a street; it is now dark

Susan is on a doorstep talking to a balding, unshaven, shabby figure, peering out at her suspiciously through a half open door.

SUSAN Hello, I'm canvassing for Mr Blyberg. Mr Blyberg is the only candidate on both sides of the Peace Line, and so . . . Would you like a leaflet? (*She fumbles in her bag.*) Do you think you might vote for Mr Blyberg. (*Silence*) Have you – Well, have you any questions?

Silence. The door slowly starts to close.

SUSAN Well – have you any problems?

The door slowly re-opens.

O'NEILL Problems?
SUSAN Well . . . yes.

O'Neill reaches out, and slowly grips her wrist.

A NIGHT OF THE CAMPAIGN

O'NEILL If you want *problems*, I'll show you some sodding problems. Come in.

They go inside.

O'NEILL (*in a low voice*) Look at this.

The room is a jumble of stoves, toasters, small television sets, light fittings, loudspeakers, opera glasses, bicycle wheels, a few oil paintings, etc. etc. Nothing looks new, but nothing looks decrepit; everything has been lovingly cleaned and dusted.

SUSAN Yes? What?

O'NEILL Wholesale robbery.

SUSAN A . . . a . . . break in?

O'NEILL Ought to be a law against it.

SUSAN (*bewildered*) But there is . . . isn't there? I'll report it.

O'NEILL You? You? *You* won't do nothing. None of yer. I've got letters here. Long as yer arm. James Prior. Heard of him? Charles Haughey. Sod-all use *he* was. (*His voice rising*) I could show you. So-called men of importance. But do you get satisfaction? No! Politicians, I shit 'em! A man tries to carry on a legitimate business . . .

Louis enters: younger and fatter than O'Neill, and with a sly expression. O'Neill suddenly looks anxious.

LOUIS What the hell are you screaming about?

O'NEILL No need for you. I'm talking to the lady. Sod off.

LOUIS (*ignoring this*) He getting at you? He's bloody mad.

O'NEILL (*to Susan*) My brother. Ignore him. If we take no notice he'll go away.

LOUIS (*grinning*) Got you in to see this load of rubbish, has he?

O'NEILL (*screams*) Will you get out! Get out! (*He switches on a radio*) There. Listen to that.

SUSAN Yes . . .?

O'NEILL Well?

SUSAN (*straining*) Can't hear anything.

O'NEILL No. That's the point, isn't it. Doesn't work. I gave fifty for that and no a squeak out of it! Complaints. Write that down.

SUSAN Well, I . . .

O'NEILL Complaints. Go on. Put it down. Consumer problems. My name's O'Neill. Write it all down.

SUSAN (*scribbling*) Yes . . . I . . . but what am I supposed –

O'NEILL Don't argue. Now look at this. Thirty I paid for this.

Begins pulling at hose of a vacuum cleaner buried deep in the pile

LOUIS (*winking at Susan*) He's dulally. Take no notice.
O'NEILL *Will you* – Ignorant git.
LOUIS Ratbag.
O'NEILL Mind like a sewer.
LOUIS Look who's talking.

O'Neill turns angrily to Susan.

O'NEILL Got that? Bloody well write it down! Don't stand there gawping!

Susan is startled into writing again.

O'NEILL Where's that knitting machine? One fifty I gave for this, and it's got some nuts missing.
LOUIS (*winks at Susan*) Nuts!
O'NEILL Look, I've already told you, last warning.

Covers his embarrassment by snatching Susan's papers from her hands.

O'NEILL Right. See where we've got to. What the frigging 'ell is this? Don't they teach you to write English at your school –

Stops, actually now reading, stunned.

O'NEILL Hundred and fifty pounds? Who said that? (*Frightened*) You out of your mind? One pound fifty, I said. And here! – *fifty p* I said.

O'Neill grabs the pen from Susan and scratches at the paper

O'NEILL Now we'll have to start again from the beginning.
SUSAN No, really, I –
LOUIS (*still laughing*) Can't alter that. Official document.
O'NEILL (*pleading*) Louis, don't keep on.
LOUIS I'll stand up in court.
O'NEILL You can't – (*To Susan*) Can he? Go against your own brother.
LOUIS Have to tell the truth.
O'NEILL It's like Mammy always said. Can't be trusted. Will you stop it?
LOUIS Oh. Oh, (*winking at Susan*) now he starts his fits. Just watch.

O'NEILL *(desperately)* I don't – I don't – stop it.
LOUIS We ought to have put you away in Purdyburn. That's what Mammy always said!

O'Neill, weeping, makes a frantic dash at Louis.

O'NEILL Get back in there. Interfering in my conversation.
LOUIS *(dancing out of reach)* Loony!
O'NEILL *(pursuing Louis)* Get back!

Louis slipping round behind Susan.

LOUIS Lo-o-ny!

Scene fades on the brothers in pursuit around a bewildered, scared Susan, objects scattering.

10 Sean's Room. Night

Dermot, Alan, Sean and Margaret are waiting in Sean's room.

ALAN *(fidgeting and restless)* Well, where can she be?
SEAN I only left her for five minutes.
ALAN Oh. Great.

Silence.

MARGARET May I enquire, are *we* the only canvassers?
ALAN Yes!
MARGARET Oh. Pardon me for asking.
ALAN No, sorry . . . Yes. Sorry . . .
MARGARET Only we had expected *some* local support, you know.
ALAN *(muttering)* Yes. Yes. *I* expected it too . . .
MARGARET What is the point of South Belfast people coming all the way from Malone Road if there is no local support?
DERMOT *(hushing her)* Margaret.
MARGARET *(snappily)* Don't Margaret me.
DERMOT Oh . . . All right . . .

Silence.

SEAN Oh, for Christ sake, Alan! She's in no danger. There wasn't a Brit in sight.
MARGARET *(laughs)* Surely you were not suggesting the girl might be in danger from the British Army?
ALAN *(suddenly emphatic)* No, no. He wasn't Margaret.

SEAN I might. (*Nods at her coldly*) I was.
MARGARET Oh, really!
SEAN Well, they managed to kill, very efficiently, one Irish child yesterday.
MARGARET Ah, *accidentally*.
ALAN Er – Sean –
SEAN Accident?
MARGARET There was a riot – surely you heard?
SEAN The wee girl wasn't in the riot.
MARGARET No? Well, then, her mother shouldn't have let her out into the streets.
SEAN (*icily*) She was on her way home from school!
ALAN Now, Sean, drop it.
SEAN Your precious army – if you want to know – wasn't even firing proper plastic bullets.
MARGARET How do you mean?
SEAN The surgeon dug a two volt battery out of that poor kid's skull.
MARGARET What?
SEAN Oh, yes. That's your British Army! Metal batteries! Lethal! Deliberately!

Margaret is speechless.

ALAN Sean, all right. Leave it.
SEAN (*excitedly*) But how would you like your sister – or your daughter's head packed with Ever-Ready batteries – (*to Margaret*) Would *you*?
MARGARET I don't believe it, in any case.
SEAN You calling me a liar.
ALAN She's not! *Not*! (*Pleading*) Margaret.
MARGARET May I remind you that the party supports the security forces.
SEAN (*furious*) When they're blowing the heads off wee girls!
MARGARET Oh – so it's blowing off heads now!
ALAN No, no! Oh, let's all calm down!
SEAN (*mumbling, slowly down*) Well . . .

There is an uncomfortable silence.

ALAN Now, where are we off to next? (*fumbling with his clipboard*) Bombay. No, we've done Bombay.
SEAN (*muttering to himself*) Plain murder . . .
ALAN We haven't done Delhi. Have we?

Silence.

ALAN: Margaret, you could do Delhi.
DERMOT: (*hesitantly*) We d-do have the right to criticise.

Margaret, startled, glares incredulously at Dermot. He shrinks back in his chair.

MARGARET: Criticise whom?
DERMOT: The – our – army. If they're in the wrong.
MARGARET: Who says they're in the wrong?
DERMOT: (*stronger*) If we s-support them, we have the right to criticise. Fair's fair.
SEAN: Criticism? Where does that get you? The wee girl's still lying there dead.
DERMOT: Issue a statement.

Silence – everyone is taken by surprise.

ALAN: Yes, Dermot has a ... Um, Sean, could you do Dacca?
SEAN: (*explosively*) Bill Blyberg should get off his fat arse and demand a bloody enquiry!
DERMOT: No. *You* should demand an enquiry.
MARGARET: (*rising*) Oh, for heaven's sake! We're here to *canvas*, Dermot.
SEAN: (*to Alan, puzzled*) Could I?
ALAN: (*shrugs*) You're secretary of the West Belfast Alliance.
SEAN: (*getting excited*) An enquiry!
ALAN: You won't *get* an enquiry.
SEAN: But it would make a point, wouldn't it? Would you do it for me? I mean, organise it?
ALAN: (*reluctantly*) Well –
SEAN: Ah, shut up. Come on. Secretary of the West Belfast Alliance. *Demands* an enquiry! Frigging plastic bullets!
MARGARET: Aren't we forgetting something? There's been more than one killing this week.
SEAN: So?
MARGARET: We should also demand an enquiry into the soldier's death.
SEAN: But why? The provies have already claimed responsibility for that.
MARGARET: Then we should condemn it! (*mimicking Dermot*) Fair's fair.
SEAN: Jesus.
MARGARET: Why ever not? Enquiry into one and condemn the other.

SEAN Because you do not muddle up a statement in this way!
MARGARET What do you mean?
SEAN It's a separate bloody issue!
MARGARET No need to shout!
SEAN (*shouting*) I'm not shouting. I'm trying to explain, as simply as I can, the obvious fact that you're incapable of –
MARGARET I'm quite capable of understanding *one* obvious fact – this soldier's death means nothing to you. Nothing!
SEAN Oh no?

Alan has been trying to intervene, but suddenly notices that Susan has come in.

ALAN (*relieved*) Where the hell have you been?
SUSAN Canvassing . . . Why, what have you been doing?

Margaret gives a snort of irritation. Alan snatches Susan's clipboard, but Sean puts a comforting arm round her shoulders.

SEAN Where did you get to, love?
DERMOT (*to Margaret*) They're clarifying Party policy.
ALAN (*incredulously scanning her canvas return*) You've only canvassed nine houses?
SEAN (*comfortingly to Susan*) Well, nine is better than none, isn't it?
SUSAN They kept talking . . .
ALAN *They* kept talking? – And what's this?
SUSAN Consumer problems.
ALAN It's unreadable.
SUSAN Well, you see . . . they were both a bit nuts –
ALAN Will they vote for us?

Susan looks blank. Alan laughs unkindly.

ALAN Oh, sorry. You forgot to ask . . .
MARGARET (*impatiently*) Yes! Get back to business –

She grabs the leaflets and the shoebox turning to dump them on the table.

SUSAN No!

She tries to snatch the shoebox, but Margaret hangs on. The box tips. The tortoise falls out onto table.

MARGARET (*horrified*) What is this?

SUSAN A very nice old lady gave it me.
ALAN (*resigned*) Did you ask her how she was going to vote?

Susan is silent. Alan turns away in disgust.

SEAN (*giving her a hug*) Never you mind, he's a lovely monster. Wish I was so lucky. All I ever get from canvassing is two sore feet.
DERMOT Have you got a garden?

Susan, surprised, nods.

DERMOT Tortoises are very good at killing slugs. I had a little tortoise when I was a boy.
MARGARET (*wearily*) Let's return to sanity, shall we?
SEAN Sanity?
MARGARET (*drumming her fingers on the table*) The statement.
ALAN Yes. Now look, I've been thinking.
MARGARET That soldier.
ALAN Yes, I'll include the soldier! But why don't –
SEAN Who said we're including the soldier?
ALAN Oh, Sean. Let me draw up a draft, and we can all discuss it when you get back. Yes?

Silence. Then Margaret gives a snort, and turns back to Dermot, who is tickling the tortoise and grinning.

MARGARET All right, Dermot. *Canvassing*!
DERMOT (*guiltily springing to attention*) Yes.
MARGARET Rotor arm?
DERMOT Yes! (*hurriedly producing it*)
MARGARET Good.

Margaret sweeps out, Dermot scurrying after her.

SEAN She's got him well trained, hasn't she. You'd think they were married. (*picks up clipboards*)

To Susan.

SEAN Shall we give it another go, darling.
SUSAN (*to Alan, humbly*) Can I?

Alan, sprawled back in his chair, gives an exhausted 'Why ask me?' gesture.

SEAN Better leave the monster here.

Sean puts the box on the table.

SEAN Don't want anyone accusing us of carrying a concealed weapon do we. Get to it, Alan – but watch it.
ALAN Right.

Alan nods, aware of the menace behind the smile.

SEAN (*as they go*) Give the thing a name yet, have you?
SUSAN Dingsbum.
SEAN Ah. Sounds very nice.

11 Out at Divis Flats. Night

Susan passes boarded-up and vandalised shops, and graffiti and slogans on the walkways. The lights don't work. She stops in the doorway of Mrs McMahon's front-room shop.
Mrs McMahon, a large, grim woman, counting out single cigarettes onto the counter. Two youths are watching her. They notice Susan, but are more interested in the cigarettes.
A radio is on: the news.

YOUTH 1 Half the stuffings out of that'n.

Mrs McMahon substitutes another.

NEWSREADER The soldier shot two days ago in West Belfast died this morning without regaining consciousness. He is Second Lieutenant Jeremy Bentinck of the 7th Parachute Regiment. His mother, Mrs Helen Bentinck, of Dartford, Kent, said that her son had wanted to join the army from his earliest years.

Susan tries to hurry past the youths.

YOUTH 2 Jewemy loved the regiment!
YOUTH 1 No, Mummy first and wegiment second!

Roaring with laughter, they encounter Susan in the doorway. She shrinks back.

SUSAN I'm in a hurry – would you let me pass?
YOUTH 1 Who are you?
SUSAN It's none of your business.
YOUTH 1 It is our business too.
YOUTH 2 What school's that?
YOUTH 1 I don't recognise the uniform. What school is it?

SUSAN (*frightened*) Alexandra School.
YOUTH 1 Queen Alexandra?
YOUTH 2 (*laughing*) Queen Alexandra! (*grabs one of her leaflets*)
YOUTH 1 Come on Johnny, I haven't got all day to chat to her.
YOUTH 2 What's this Alliance?
YOUTH 1 (*chanting*) Sinn Fein, Sinn Fein.

He grabs at her coat lapels, when there is a thunderous crash on the counter: Mrs McMahon is wielding a dangerous-looking lump of wood.

McMAHON Leave her be, bloody hooligans! Get the hell out, will ya?

The youths flee, laughing and jeering. Susan is left, frozen, terrified.

McMAHON (*incurious*) What's a nice wee girl like you doing round a place like this?
SUSAN I . . . I'm canvassing.
McMAHON You're canvassing?
SUSAN Bill – Bill Blyberg – Alliance candidate.
McMAHON Huh!
SUSAN Yes . . . Bill Blyberg is the only candidate who speaks for both sides.
McMAHON Alliance, SDLP, Workers Party, huh!

Silence. Then she suddenly shouts.

McMAHON Do bugger all about helping the likes of me!
SUSAN (*startled*) Yes . . . Yes he would.
McMAHON (*harsh laugh*) Would he do anything to help my son?
SUSAN Like what?
McMAHON He's been in the barrack since six this morning.
SUSAN What's he doing there?
McMAHON (*incredulous*) Doing there?
SUSAN (*frightened*) Yes?
McMAHON The army lifted him! What else? Broke down the bloody door. See there!

Stabs her arm towards the door, which Susan now see is half wrenched out: the club was part of it.

McMAHON Six o'clock this morning! They dragged him out screaming, they did. Screaming, he was. Screaming Mammy! Bounced his head on the landing, down them stairs, bang, bang, bang, his poor head, all the way to the

	bottom, and they handed him to the polis and they've had him shut in the barrack from then till this and they won't let me nor his Uncle Jimmy in to see him and they won't even answer the phone! Buggers!
SUSAN	But – but why? – what did he do?
MRS McMAHON	What did he do? How do you mean? (*She stares at Susan, hard*) What age are you?
SUSAN	Si – (*lying in panic*) Eighteen.
MRS McMAHON	Do you live in this town?
SUSAN	Yes. I'm sure we could do something!
MRS McMAHON	(*sobbing angrily*) I want till know if he's seen a doctor.
SUSAN	Yes! Yes!
MRS McMAHON	I want him t'see a doctor and, you see, they won't answer the phone, they won't answer it, his Uncle Jimmy went down there and they won't tell him nothing, neither, and it's his right, he ought t'see a doctor, he has a right t'see a doctor. I want him to see a doctor.

Tears come into Susan's eyes as the wild lament goes on.

12 Sean's Room

ALAN	(*exhausted*) Surely we agreed that. Didn't we? 'Strongly demand'?
MARGARET	Yes, but couldn't 'strongly' be counterproductive?
ALAN	I don't know. I don't care. This is the third draft, I can't keep changing it!
MARGARET	I'm not asking for change –
SEAN	(*growling*) It's in. (*To Alan*) Carry on.
MARGARET	Oh, very democratic.
SEAN	Nothing to do with democracy. This is *my* statement.
MARGARET	Yes, but how many more times? It's an *Alliance* statement.
SEAN	It's a *West Belfast* Alliance statement.
MARGARET	It merely happens to *originate* from West Belfast.
SEAN	(*indignant*) It's my statement in *my* name.
MARGARET	Well – I disassociate myself from 'strongly'.
SEAN	(*muttering*) Great news. Next paragraph.
ALAN	(*reads*) 'This Association also, condemns the mindless killing' –
MARGARET	Unreservedly.
ALAN	What?
MARGARET	Unreservedly condemns. Much better.

A NIGHT OF THE CAMPAIGN

ALAN (*mechanically writing*) – 'unreservedly condemns the mindless killing' –

SEAN Oh come on. 'Condemns' is enough.

MARGARET Not at all.

SEAN Why not?

MARGARET What possible objections can you have to 'unreservedly'?

SEAN I just think 'condemns' is enough.

MARGARET No, oh no – let's have this out in the open. What's *wrong* with unreservedly?

SEAN If the British army hadn't been flying up and down that road firing off their plastic bullets that soldier wouldn't have been there to be shot at, would he?

MARGARET If there were no terrorists they wouldn't need to be on the road!

SEAN No? Perhaps if it weren't for you and your bloody Brits they'd be no terrorists. On or off the the bloody road. Ever thought of that?

MARGARET What do you mean, 'you and your bloody Brits'? You suggesting *I'm* responsible, are you? Are you? Are you?

SEAN I didn't mean you. You know I didn't.

MARGARET I think you did.

SEAN I meant, if we didn't have the British army, we wouldn't –

MARGARET I heard what you said! I demand an apology.

SEAN Apology?

SUSAN (*entering*) Everybody! Listen! I've met this woman in Divis –

ALAN (*rolling his eyes*) What did she give you? A parrot?

SUSAN Her son's been arrested!

SEAN (*angrily*) We're busy!

SUSAN But her son –

SEAN Yes. It happens all the time – *please* –

MARGARET Not often enough, if you ask me!

SEAN (*furious*) Lady, you want an apology from me? You can –

He gives a crude gesture which shocks Margaret.

SEAN It's you – In my opinion its people like you, who cause all the problems of – of – Oh, cut to the end, Alan, cut to the bloody end!

SUSAN She wants him to see a doctor.

MARGARET Wait a minute! Is he trying to cut the soldier entirely?

SEAN 'Course not! I was asking him to read out the final paragraph –
SUSAN Alan, I promised –
MARGARET Oh! Yes! So we avoid all discussion of 'unreservedly'!
SEAN Nothing of the sort!
MARGARET Is 'unreservedly' *in*? Just tell me!
SUSAN (*whimpering*) Alan –
SEAN Jesus, Alan. What is she screaming about? Did I say –
ALAN (*shouts*) I've had enough. I – I – shut up, Sean! *Shut up!* All of you! Sit down! Listen. Enough's enough. I've got to get this statement out within two hours at most if we're to have a hope of catching the morning editions! We've already wasted half that time. Are you all mad? Don't you realise? I've got to get back from here to headquarters, pick up a typewriter, get a typist, get the copies typed, run them all round, one by one, to the bloody news offices – and then, *then*, I've got to run back to headquarters to duplicate a general press release for the local rags – What do you think I am? Superman? It can't be done! It won't be done! Not the way you're carrying on. Either you accept the thing now – as it is! Or it bloody well doesn't go out at all! Well?
MARGARET (*A stunned silence*) Was it really necessary to swear?
SEAN Get out, Alan! Yes. It's accepted! Clear off.
MARGARET But what about –
SEAN 'Unreservedly'! All right. You win.
ALAN All right, all right, Susan!

Sean hustles Alan out of the door and Susan follows.

SEAN Will you be in time? Will you manage, do you think?
ALAN (*impatient*) Yes, yes. Don't panic.
SUSAN (*whimpering*) Alan . . .
ALAN Yes, yes!?
SEAN But what about the typing?
ALAN I'll get it to Muriel!
SEAN Muriel?
ALAN She's duty typist for the evening.
SUSAN Alan . . .
ALAN Look, unless you can type, shut up. You concentrate on your tortoise.

They both realise she hasn't got the tortoise.

SUSAN Oh!

She pushes back through them up the stairs. Reaching the landing, Susan finds Dermot emerging apologetically from room, proferring the tortoise and shoebox.
Susan, relieved, grabs them, gives Dermot a hurried kiss and hurries down again.
Margaret, still cross, finds Dermot motionless, a beautiful smile upon his face, staring after Susan down the stairs.

MARGARET Come on, Dermot, we're leaving. Rotor arm.
DERMOT Oh, damn it! (*He searches feverishly*) It's such a silly tiny little thing. Keep taking it out and putting it back – Oh –
MARGARET *Find it!*

She hurries down the stairs, with Dermot following, still vainly searching. Outside, Alan's car is just pulling away.

MARGARET Stop! . . .

But he zooms off. Margaret turns to Dermot, her hands feverishly intertwining with his as she joins in the search.

MARGARET Find it . . . Do you want us to be stranded here with this maniac?

She notices a bemused Sean at her elbow.
Margaret, Dermot and Sean trailing agitatedly down the dark street.

MARGARET Try it without the rotor arm, you never know. (*She tries starting the car*) Where's the nearest phone?
SEAN No phone round here.
MARGARET But there must be *something*! Some transport!
SEAN Jesus, what do you expect me to do? Rustle you up an army helicopter?
MARGARET (*despairing*) Oh, Dermot.

Dermot, shrinking, begins another despairing flutter through his pockets.

MARGARET What about *taxis*?
SEAN Not unless you're a Provie.
MARGARET Provie?
SEAN There's Provie taxis. Bugger all else.
MARGARET (*looking at the empty street, and sighing*) Bed and breakfast?

SEAN Are you joking? You'll have to hoof it. Or you could come back to my place.
MARGARET *Your* place?
SEAN (*grins*) I'll make you comfy – I'll surprise you.

Margaret glares at him, suspiciously. Hesitates, sighs.

MARGARET Oh, all right. . . . lead the way.

13 Alliance Headquarters

SUSAN (*coming in with Alan*) Habeas Corpus!
ALAN Doesn't exist.
SUSAN Yes it does. The Habeas Corpus Act, 1679. I did it in History – Who holds the body.
ALAN The Royal Ulster Constabulary. And they'll stick to it.
SUSAN They can't.
ALAN They will. Look, find me the handbook.
SUSAN It's in the constitution. It was only passed because one fat lord –
ALAN Will you shut up.
SUSAN Then what do I do?
ALAN Ring Police Headquarters.

Susan goes to the phone.

ALAN Not now!
SUSAN When?
ALAN Sometime.
SUSAN And what's happening to her boy all this 'sometime'?

But Alan is already half-way out the door, carrying his typewriter and paper. She grabs the telephone directory and follows him.

SUSAN We're here to help people. Not make stupid statements!

14 Outside Philip Pelham's House. Later

ALAN Ah Muriel – a little statement for you to type. Only take a minute – Anything wrong?
MURIEL (*whispering*) Oh, no. Only . . . Philip's in. Having dinner. Er, could you come in rather quietly . . .?

Alan and Susan enter a dark, oppressive room, with university mementoes on the walls, a heavy glass-fronted bookcase and a well-stocked drinks cabinet.

A NIGHT OF THE CAMPAIGN

MURIEL (*whispering nervously*) If you'll just give me a moment.
SUSAN Can I use the phone?
MURIEL (*whispering*) Of course.

She exits hurriedly, while Alan lays his work out on the table.

ALAN You don't give up, do you.
SUSAN (*busy thumbing through the telephone directory*) No!

A heavy voice is heard coming from down the passageway, English, well-educated.

PHILIP Who was it then? I asked a question.

There is a distant clink of plates, an inaudible reply.

PHILIP (*sharper*) All right, I'm probably not interested in your answer, but I do like to *hear* it.

Inaudible reply. Susan has started to dial.

PHILIP Very well then, it *was* nothing. Now we know. Simple enough, wasn't it? But I don't need two *knives*, do I? Why is it you can never lay a table decently. (*voice sinking*) And where is the . . .
MURIEL I made you a pot of tea –
PHILIP (*more nastily*) Yes, yes, but I prefer a proper drink. Do you mind?

Heavy footsteps approach down the passage, then the door is flung open. Philip appears. He stops, surprised to see Susan and Alan. Now he stands in the doorway, staring, frowning, a frightening figure. Susan holds the telephone, almost as a shield.

PHILIP Ah . . . so you're the nothing, are you? Welcome, nothings. (*He takes the receiver from Susan, listens then offers it back to her*) It's the police.

Alan grabs it.

ALAN (*very embarrassed*) Hello. I'm telephoning on behalf of Councillor Bill Blyberg, the Alliance candidate for West Belfast.
PHILIP Oh my God. Oh yes, of course, the Alliance! I thought I'd seen you somewhere before.
ALAN Yes, we're . . . making enquiries about a boy you're holding.
PHILIP Yes, you've been here, haven't you?

ALAN (*sweating*) Yes! (*to Susan, gesticulating wildly*) What's his name?

PHILIP (*making for the drinks cabinet*) Alliance! I might have guessed. My wife, she's addicted to lost causes.

SUSAN Malachi.

PHILIP What the hell does *she* know about politics? (*pouring himself an Irish whisky*) What does anyone know? Who but a born again idiot could want to dip their nose in that unholy brew? Eh?

Susan hands the McMahon details, on a scrap of paper, to Alan.

SUSAN Malachi Pius McMahon.

ALAN (*into receiver*) Sorry. Just a second.

PHILIP But she – ah, she has an unfailing instinct for lost causes you kna.

ALAN Malachi Pius *McMahon*.

PHILIP (*raises whisky bottle to Susan*) This. This is the only tolerable brew in this Godforsaken country.

ALAN Yes, McMahon.

PHILIP We should snaffle up your whisky and run! Leave you maniacs to fight it out here amongst yourself. (*Leaning over Alan*) Eh?

ALAN (*nods, grins weakly*) One – oh – five Divis Walk.

PHILIP It'll come to that in the end. It's inevitable! Take what you want, says God – and *pay* for it! Isn't that what the Spanish say?

SUSAN (*in a panic*) How should *I* know?

PHILIP We've taken all we wanted from the world, have we not? Painted the map red! And now – by God! – we're paying for it. Statements!

Contemptuously sweeping up Alan's sheet from table.

PHILIP Enquiry! Yes, that all that's left to us. Statements, enquiries! 'Mindless Killing'!Huh! Who's mindless? The poor bugger who left his brains spewed out upon the pavement, *he's* mindless. Enquiry!

Flinging down the statement, beginning to move out of the room, shouting down the passageway.

PHILIP My wife would like an enquiry. Into my drinking habits. I tell her there's no need. Drinking is a logical response to a maniac situation. Isn't it? She and her 'mindless'

Alliance, *they'd* drive a man to drink – you merry little do-gooder you.

Alan, writing on a scrap of paper the details he's been given.

ALAN Yes, could you tell me – has he seen a doctor?
PHILIP (*reappearing, eyes agleam*) Doctor? Oh no. And he won't Sonny, believe me!

Exits again, manically.

PHILIP (*overheard in the passageway*) So? Have you enrolled your infant nothings in the conspiracy? Eh? Charming! Soon you'll have your paraplegic foot painters! And your League of Battered Wives! And a coach-load or two of loonies from your Therapy Self-Help Group, eh? All pounding at the bloody door, telling me to abhor the demon drink. It's my house! My money pays for it! I slave away daily pumping English Lit into Irish donkeys just to finance your idiocies? *Do* I?

Silence.
Susan and Alan, look at each other, shocked. Philip re-enters, bristling with rage.

PHILIP No response from the little wifey, of course. Never is. She'd lose a talking contest with a Trappist monk –
SUSAN (*fiercely*) Shut up!
PHILIP (*stunned*) What did you say?
SUSAN I said shut up! You pig!

Philip looks suddenly shrunken, a hurt little boy.

PHILIP I see ... very pleasant ... I ... (*He crashes the glass down upon the table.*) Tell my loving wife I'm out for the remainder of the evening.

He goes out, slamming the front door.

ALAN (*groan*) Susan!
SUSAN I couldn't take it any longer.

Muriel appears at the door.

MURIEL (*breathless*) What that Philip?
ALAN Yes. I'm sorry.
MURIEL Oh ... I expect he ... Yes, he *did* have an appointment ... I ... (*moves quickly to table*) Is this it? (*She picks up the*

'statement' from table) Oh no, it's not too long. It won't take a jif. How many copies do we need?

ALAN Half a dozen.

MURIEL Oh. (*Laughs, breathless*) Yes. Stupid of me. (*She fusses with her carbon paper, head down*) Yes ... we caught him on a b – (*She stops, then laughs determinedly and begins to type*) Well! Shall we win the election?

SUSAN (*eagerly, comfortingly*) Yes!

Muriel looks up, startled, at Susan, then grins haphazardly at Alan. She and Alan both know she had asked an absurd question.

ALAN (*gently*) We should get ten per cent.

Susan opens her mouth to protest, but is shrivelled by a glare from Alan.

MURIEL (*typing, brightly*) Well, that would be a moral victory, wouldn't it? In a way.

ALAN Oh yes.

Alan smiles comfortingly at Muriel, who carries on typing, head down. Susan looks on, concerned and upset.

Later, after waving goodbye to Muriel who now looks radiantly happy, they bundle their equipment into the car and speed off.

ALAN You know what he did – your 'boy'? First, he's not a boy, he's twenty-eight. Second, he escaped from the Royal Victoria Hospital while he was there from Crumlin Road Gaol, having his ears syringed. He dived through a plate-glass window, hijacked a passing car, nearly ran over an elderly shopper, and crashed into a road-block in Newtownards. He's been on the run for two and a half years. And he hasn't been exactly idle while on the run ...

15 Alliance Headquarters

Back at the Alliance headquarters, exhausted after delivering their statement to offices all round Belfast, Susan shrinks from making the necessary telephone call.

SUSAN (*whimpering*) It's *your* job. You should –

ALAN Oh! Not again – get on with it.

A NIGHT OF THE CAMPAIGN

SUSAN How should I start?
ALAN You pick up the receiver, you dial.
SUSAN Please!
ALAN No.

She lifts receiver, starts dialing, while he winds statement on to the duplicator. Almost immediately she looks up, pleased.

SUSAN There's no reply!

He turns, looks. She scowls, cradles the receiver again to her ear. Her face drops. Mrs McMahon is obviously answering. She speaks very timidly, tentatively.

SUSAN Mrs McMahon, it's me . . . Susan. The Alliance party . . . yes. Yes, we managed to get through, and he's okay. He's seen a doctor, and he's perfectly okay . . . yes . . . no, it was no bother – but, Mrs McMahon, I'm afraid they're going to charge him with . . . Escaping while under lawful arrest . . . Membership . . . Mrs McMahon . . . possession of firearms . . . and . . . attempted murder, Mrs McMahon. I'm sorry, I'm really sorry . . . Oh, not at all. It was nothing . . . yes, goodbye.

Susan replaces the receiver, puzzled.

ALAN What did she say?
SUSAN All right.
ALAN Just all right?
SUSAN Yes. That's all right . . . just as long as they're not beating him up.

Susan sinks down onto the chair, and mechanically cradles the shoebox.

ALAN Well, at least now she knows . . .

He turns back to the duplicator but the machine won't start.

ALAN Oh, Christ . . . (*He thumps it*) Well, it's nothing to get upset about . . .

She does not reply.

ALAN She's probably got a few more stuck away. Maze or somewhere . . .

Tears start to trickle down Susan's face.

ALAN Now what is there to cry about?
SUSAN (*weeping*) Dingsbum ...
ALAN Oh, all right. Talk to your bloody tortoise.
SUSAN (*furiously*) I might as well! There's no use talking to you. You don't understand!
ALAN I do understand.
SUSAN (*up on her feet*) You just laugh at it all!
ALAN I do not.
SUSAN You did! Him being charged and his mother only worrying in case he'd been beaten up! That's not funny!
ALAN No. It's not. *If* he hasn't been beaten up.
SUSAN (*shaken*) What do you mean?
ALAN Oh Sue. (*Going to her*) They're not going to *tell* us if they have. Are they? 'Yes, he turning a nice shade of black and blue, sorry, Mrs McMahon ...'

Silence. He shrugs, shamefaced.

ALAN That's why I laughed.

He hesitantly puts his hand to her shoulder, but she grinds her head against his chest, moaning. Alan embarrassed, and not knowing what to do, pats her.

ALAN I'm sorry Sue – I shouldn't have said – they probably haven't –
SUSAN It's all bloody laughing! There were boys at Mrs McMahon's even laughing at the death of that soldier!
ALAN All right yes.
SUSAN And that shit Philip!
ALAN Yes, but you mustn't blame me.
SUSAN No, but it's all torturing and – killing! And laughing about it!
ALAN I did try to warn you off.
SUSAN Yes, Alan, you did.
ALAN The moment you arrived. I said, didn't I ...
SUSAN Yes ... you did Alan.

She raised her blind, unhappy face to him, lips parting. Alan freezes, shocked.

SUSAN (*opening her eyes*) What?

Alan, stiffly loosening his hold on her.

ALAN Let's cool it.

A NIGHT OF THE CAMPAIGN

Susan stepping back, confused, faintly.

SUSAN   I'm sorry . . . I . . .

ALAN   (*awkwardly*) It's nearly eleven. It's really time I took you home. It's long past your bed-time. I can leave the duplicating till I get back.

He jangles his car keys.

ALAN   Well, come on. Let's get out of this dump.

She is crying.

ALAN   You'll have forgotten all this, in the morning. What are you crying about *now*?

SUSAN   Nothing.

ALAN   If it's nothing, stop it! Your parents will think I've been assaulting you or something. Stop it!

SUSAN   Just take me home.

ALAN   (*stares*) What are you up to?

And Susan's crying suddenly shrivels. She turns to go but he blocks her.

SUSAN   What do you mean?

ALAN   Why did you come here?

SUSAN   It's nothing to do with you. I would have come . . . (*Tears suddenly overwhelm her*) . . . Mr Pattison, in Maths, made a joke about it. He said you were Big Chief Alliance for the night. (*She weeps on miserably*)

ALAN   Sue. You've been really stupid.

SUSAN   (*suddenly shouting*) Yes! I *was*! I'm embarrassing you.

ALAN   No, no, Sue. You're not embarrassing me . .

SUSAN   Take me home! I won't lay a finger on you! I'll sit in the back seat!

ALAN   Oh God, this is ridiculous. You've got to be sensible. We *can't*. It's not right. Teachers can't.

SUSAN   (*indignant*) But you're *not* a teacher! You said so!

ALAN   I know I did, but I *am* a teacher. I'm in a teacher situation. It'll only cause embarrassment . . .

SUSAN   (*triumph*) Ah!

ALAN   I mean to *you*! If you get caught up – in this sort of entanglement. (*Pleading*) I like you, Sue. You know I do. You're practically a femme fatale, do you know that?

SUSAN   Femme fatale? What's that?

ALAN   It's – ah, it doesn't matter. When the time is right you'll set Belfast ablaze from end to end.

SUSAN   Aren't there enough people doing that already?

ALAN   (*grabbing her feverishly*) You know what I mean. You're too young – people would talk, your parents would flip their lids. So, I can't even though I do –

He sighs. Susan looks at him. He tries to complete the word 'like', but no sound emerges. His head is inclining towards her, seemingly of its own volition. Their lips meet.
The kiss is finally broken by Alan. He holds Susan to him; she, eyes closed, contentedly nestles her head under his chin. He gazes desparingly up at the ceiling.

ALAN   ... and I'm supposed to be getting out the general press release.

SUSAN   Doesn't matter ...

ALAN   It does! Sit down. Sit there. Relax.

Alan almost knocks over transistor, switching it on.
He gives the duplicator a frenzied swipe and it responds, and starts cranking out copies.

ALAN   Ah! Right, you bugger!

Susan sits watching him.

NEWSREADER   And now the news at 11 o'clock. The controversy over that gas pipe line from the Republic of Ireland continues. The Chairman of the local Councillor's Association has called on the Government to forget the whole deal. 'It would be dangerous' he alleged, 'for the people of Ulster to rely on' what he calls 'Green Gas'. He went on to suggest that North Sea gas should be piped across St George's Channel to Northern Ireland. (*Pause*) The police are tonight searching for a sixteen year old schoolgirl, Susan Watson, who went missing from her home in the Stranmillis area of South Belfast earlier this evening. She was wearing her school uniform of beige blouse, bottle-green pullover and skirt, and the police are asking anyone who can give information to contact Belfast Police on Belfast 694951 ...

Alan freezes. Susan is blissfully unaware.

ALAN   Sue!

SUSAN   What does it mean?

ALAN (*stopping the duplicator*) Christ!
SUSAN What are you doing?
ALAN 'Phoning your mother! Didn't you tell them where you were going?
SUSAN Yes!

Susan furiously tries to grab the receiver from him.

ALAN (*still fending off Susan*) Hello, Mrs Watson, Susan's here.

Susan gives up in disgust.

ALAN She's with me. Alan Smith. She's quite safe, Mrs Watson! She –

His speech is cut short by a torrent, from Mrs Watson. Alan hastily thrusts the receiver at Susan. She snatches it, with a murderous scowl.

SUSAN Mummy! What are you playing at!
NEWSREADER (*carrying on meanwhile*) The death of a child in West Belfast yesterday after being hit by a plastic bullet continues to provoke comment. Independent councillor, Frank Field, has accused the army of criminal negligence and demanded that the soldier responsible be charged with murder . . .
SUSAN Of course I'm all right! Why did you call the police in?
NEWSREADER Provisional Sinn Fein have called for the army to be removed altogether, where, they say, they are a constant and dangerous provocation to the nationalist population . . .
SUSAN *Alliance Party Headquarters*! Can't you listen when I tell you anything.
NEWSREADER The Secretary of the West Belfast Alliance Party . . .

Alan turns towards the transistor.

NEWSREADER . . . has called for a full judicial enquiry . . .
ALAN (*awed*) Good God . . .
SUSAN (*yelling*) Canvassing! Canvassing!
NEWSREADER The Alliance statement also condemns what they call 'the mindless killing of a young soldier in the same area this week'.
ALAN (*in ecstasy*) We did it – My Christ! We've done it . . . They ran it . . . Oh, my God – Susan!
NEWSREADER 'The soldier, 2nd Lieutenant Jeremy Bentinck of the 7th

Parachute Regiment, died early this morning from wounds received in an accident.'

Alan switches off. During the following he begins scribbling away at the far end of the table from Susan.

SUSAN (*shouting*) *No!* Of course I wasn't at Party Headquarters *all* the time. How *could* I be, if I was canvassing? (*Appalled*) But what was the point of ringing 'Ammesty International'? I said Alliance! Of course they wouldn't know anything about me there! Oh, Mummy, what have you got in your head, sawdust? Oh I'm sorry, but, look, I was helping people and I didn't have time to phone. I was helping a woman whose son has been arrested! And we've been writing a very important statement, about the whole situation – And, I met a very nice old woman and she gave me a tortoise ... (*her voice falters, checking*) Yes ... a tortoise. Only a little one ... but Mummy! Yes! I know I'm shouting, because you're so stupid. So stop worrying, I'm all right, goodnight. (*slams down the receiver*) Oh, what a bloody mess. I'll kill her.

ALAN You heard, did you? The *statement*. The *news!* Listen. I'm expanding the general press release, slipping in a bit about that McMahon business. Try and get a follow-up on tomorrow's news!

Then noticing Susan's distress.

ALAN Well, what's wrong with you?
SUSAN (*choked*) She – she won't – let me bring home *Di -ings -bum,* she – she says we don't want that dirty thing in the house.
ALAN Oh, ... Well, don't worry. We'll think of something.
SUSAN That settles it, doesn't it!
ALAN Settles what?
SUSAN I *have* to come with you now.
ALAN What? Are you mad? I've got to return you to your home, or we'll have the police round here.
SUSAN You can do what you like. If I can't come with you, I'll sleep here! On the bloody floor.

She thumps herself down in a chair, folds her arms. Silence.

ALAN We have mice. Did you know that? If I don't run you back, I'll probably get done for kidnapping ... (*Susan is silent*) I can look after Dingsby for you ...

SUSAN Dingsbum.
ALAN All right then, Dingsbum.

Silence.

SUSAN You don't know how.
ALAN I'll read books.

Abruptly, she reaches for the box, still not looking at him, deposits it in his lap, and goes to the door.

ALAN Sue . . .

She turns and looks at him sternly.

ALAN You could come and show me how. Sometime . . . Tomorrow, say?

A long look passes between them. She allows him a glimmer of a smile, turns and goes out. After a few minutes hesitation, Alan follows her out. As the door closes behind him, we see a poster which reads 'Alliance unites people'.

Coursework assignments for GCSE

Intensive Care

1 This play has a title which could have more than one meaning. What is the medical meaning, and what could it suggest besides that?
2 From the evidence of the play, write a description of Midgley's father. He may have been a bit malicious, but what were his good points?
3 Midgley went to see his father most weekends. Should he have done more? Should old people be cared for by their relatives, or should they be looked after by the state? What are your own views on this question?
4 On page 5 Alan Bennett points out that he got on well with his father, yet he says, 'parents aren't normal people and nor are children'. What does he mean by this? Now think about the people you know. Write an argument between a boy or girl and a parent, in which neither can see that the other has got a point.
5 Midgley and his family seem a fairly 'normal' bunch, but they're not exactly happy together. What's been going wrong, and can any of it be put right?
6 Imagine that Midgley and his wife have come to you for advice on how to repair their damaged relationship. Write two separate conversations: one in which you listen to him and advise him, the other in which you do the same for her.
7 Imagine that after the play Midgley leaves home. Tell the story of what happens then.
8 Write a conversation which takes place in the hospital waiting room, between Aunty Kitty and Uncle Ernest. Before you start, consider Aunty Kitty's attitudes particularly towards people of different races. Do you approve of her views?
9 Read the scene in which the teachers at Midgley's school meet the parents and then write a scene about a parents' night at your own school.

10 Midgley's dream, in which he is a small boy out with his parents, is very strange, but dreams often are. Describe one of your own dreams and then do a painting or a drawing to go with it.
11 In this play the characters often talk 'past' each other – they don't listen to anyone else, and they simply speak their own thoughts. Find one of the scenes where this happens and then write a scene of your own in which two of your friends talk 'past' each other. Try to make it funny.

The Flip Side of Dominick Hide

12 This play is set in the future. What things have changed? How is life different in Dominick's world?
13 In Dominick's world people still speak English, but they talk differently. What is it that makes their speech different from ours? Give some examples to show what you mean.
14 Dominick is surprised and puzzled by many things in the world of 1980. Make a list of some of these.
15 Imagine that you, like Dominick, live in the future, and that you decide to visit the world your great-grandparents lived in. You fly back in time, and land in the place where you yourself actually now live. What surprises you? What frightens you? What fascinates you? Tell it as a story, starting with your feelings as you land in this unknown place.
16 Now imagine you are going to visit your great grandson in his world in the future. Tell the story of your journey through time and space, and of what happens when you get there.
17 Imagine that Jane keeps a diary. Write the entries, from her first meeting with Dominick to the birth of her baby. Remember that Dominick is a mystery to her. Use the facts in the play as your basis, and try to imagine how the other people will behave towards her.
18 Imagine that you are Dominick's son. Jane, your mother, often talks about your father, but she can't tell the truth because she doesn't understand it. Write one of the conversations you have with her: you are putting the questions and she is giving evasive and confusing answers.

INTENSIVE CARE

19 Dominick's sudden disappearances make his mother and Ava very uneasy. Write a conversation in which they discuss the problem and try to hit on a way of solving it. And remember – they don't speak quite as we do: their language is cooler and briefer and more formal than ours.
20 Let's suppose that you are creating a time capsule which will be placed in your local town hall and opened by future generations in the year 2080. What will you put into it? Think of things which, though ordinary objects now, may seem strange to people in the future.
21 Now let's suppose you are going to travel back long ago in history. Decide when and where you are going back to (it does not have to be Britain) and tell the story.

Looking for Vicky

22 The story of this play is almost all told from the point of view of Clare. What do we know about the other characters? Make headings for Philippa, Red, and Derek and list what we know of them.
23 On page 114 Jane Hollowood says it might be interesting to explore Derek's inner world. Imagine that he puts his hopes and fears into a diary which he writes on the train going to and from his work in the City. Write a series of morning and evening entries over several days.
24 Clare is at first terrified of Red, but she later discovers that he has troubles of his own, and that his life has gone wrong. Imagine how and why he originally left home, and tell his story. Continue it, if you like, past the point where the play ends.
25 Imagine the scene in which Philippa and Red first meet. Write the conversation in which they begin to find each other attractive.
26 Write your own version of Philippa's diary, from the first meeting with Red to the last moments of the play when she and Clare return home.
27 Imagine that Clare writes to a friend about her family problems, and asks advice both about what to do with Philippa and about her own life. Write that letter and the reply, making the most helpful suggestions you can.
28 Write a story or a play about a series of threatening phone calls.

A Night of the Campaign

29 Why is Alan so uneasy about Susan's insistence on working for the Alliance Party? There could be several reasons, so list as many as you can.

30 Is it fair to say that Susan's parents come across as particularly stupid and unsympathetic in this play? Give evidence from the play to back up your opinion.

31 Do you have political disagreements with your parents? Write a conversation in which you and they disagree over some current problem. And remember – 'political' doesn't just refer to the main national political parties – it can cover anything from defence to the national health service, from trade unions to the treatment of minority groups.

32 Imagine the scene when Susan finally gets home to her parents. Turn it into a short play.

33 What happens when Alan and Susan next have a chance to talk outside the classroom? How will being in school affect the way they speak to each other? Write their conversation.

34 If Alan and Susan both kept diaries, how do you think their accounts of the events of the play would differ? Write the entry each would have made that night. Look carefully at the events, and decide what each would emphasise from the night's activities.

35 This play was written in 1985. What major events have happened in Belfast since then – and has the basic situation changed? If it has, then how? See if you can find any current newspaper stories which echo the events of the play.

36 What other cities in the world are divided, as Belfast is, by religion? Investigate the situation in another city which is similarly divided, and list the parallels.

37 Write a speech by an Ulster Protestant, explaining why he hates the Catholics. Then write a speech by a Catholic, giving his reasons why he believes his cause is justified. You will need to do some research into recent history for this – look particularly at what happened in 1916.

38 In his introduction the author says that some people in the Alliance Party attacked him for 'having made fun of good people who were doing their utmost "to save Northern

Ireland from a bloody civil war"'. Do you think these people have a case?

General questions

39 Which play did you like best? What made you want to keep reading to the end?
40 Choose one of these four plays and explain in detail how it would have to be changed if it were to be presented on the stage instead of on television. Look at each scene – and remember the physical limitations which the stage entails. Quick cutting from one place to another and back again is out of the question, unless you divide the stage, play with the lighting, and ask the audience to play at make-believe.
41 All of these plays deal with conflict between different generations. Take any three examples of parents and children here and show how their attitudes differ.
42 In a short television play only a few characters can come across with any depth. Most of the minor characters exist as a background for the principal ones. Choose three minor characters and show how the authors have drawn them, just giving enough information for them to seem real.
43 Write a play of your own. Begin by writing its story, then decide what your characters are going to be like, and then whether your play is going to be for the stage, television, cinema or the radio. And remember – if you are writing for radio you must always allow for the fact that the audience can see nothing – everything must be suggested by the dialogue.

Additional coursework assignments by Margaret Mackey.

Wider Reading

H G WELLS, *The Time Machine*,
 A traveller flashes forward in time to the year 802701, where people are divided into two classes: the Morlocks, who live and work in caves under the earth, and the Eloi, who are graceful, idle, and pleasure-seeking.

VIRGINIA WOOLF, *Orlando*,
 A delightful fantasy in which the hero, an English aristocrat, moves through four centuries from Elizabethan times to the twentieth century. But he also changes – from a man of action into a poet, then into a woman of fashion and a Victorian lady.

MARGARET MAHY, *Aliens in the Family*,
 An alien is pursued by a gang of rival aliens who want to steal the secrets of his civilisation, and he disguises himself and takes refuge in a New Zealand family. Comic, but with a serious emotional dimension. Suitable for less able readers.

ALAN GARNER, *Red Shift*,
 A very difficult book on a first reading, but gradually its riddles reveal the complex interlocking of three different events at three different times in history which occur in the same place. Violent, vivid, haunting.

BERLIE DOHERTY, *White Peak Farm*,
 A series of stories about family life on a Derbyshire farm. The narrator is a girl; the atmosphere entirely realistic.

J D SALINGER, *The Catcher in the Rye*,
 The greatest classic of adolescence this century. The young narrator is painfully honest about the bogusness of the adult world; fourteen-year-olds of both sexes will passionately identify with him.

ALAN BENNETT, *A Writer in Disguise*,
 Five more plays by our best tv dramatist, with extracts from his diary kept while their production was in progress, and an essay on how the writer turns life into art.

FRANK ORMSBY (ED), *Northern Windows*,
  A collection of Olster childhoods from a number of autobiographies. An excellent introduction to the politics, history and culture of Northern Ireland.

PETER CARTER, *Under Goliath*,
  The title is the nickname for the giant shipyard crane which dominates the skyline of Protestant East Belfast. A dramatic story of the Troubles.

JOAN LINGARD, *The Twelfth Day of July*,
  The tale of a friendship which endures despite the barricades of war-torn Belfast. Like Romeo and Juliet, the hero and heroine presist in their relationship in the face of family opposition on both sides.

Longman Imprint Books
General Editor: Michael Marland CBE MA

Titles in the series
There is a Happy Land Keith Waterhouse
The Human Element Stan Barstow
Conflicting Generations Five television scripts
A Sillitoe Selection *edited by* Michael Marland
***Late Night on Watling Street and other stories** Bill Naughton
Black Boy Richard Wright
Scene Scripts Seven television plays
Ten Western Stories *edited by* C. E. J. Smith
Loves, Hopes and Fears *edited by* Michael Marland
Cider with Rosie Laurie Lee
Goalkeepers are Crazy Brian Glanville
A James Joyce Selection *edited by* Richard Adams
Out of the Air Five radio plays *edited by* Alfred Bradley
Scene Scripts Two Five television plays
Caribbean Stories *edited by* Michael Marland
An Isherwood Selection *edited by* Geoffrey Halson
A Thomas Hardy Selection *edited by* Geoffrey Halson
The Experience of Parenthood *edited by* Chris Buckton
The Experience of Love *edited by* Michael Marland
Twelve War Stories *edited by* John L. Foster
A Roald Dahl Selection *edited by* Roy Blatchford
A D H Lawrence Selection *edited by* Geoffrey Halson
I'm the King of the Castle Susan Hill
Sliding Leslie Norris
Still Waters Three television plays by Julia Jones
Scene Scripts Three Four television plays *edited by* Roy Blatchford
Television Comedy Scripts Five scripts *edited by* Roy Blatchford
Juliet Bravo Five television scripts
Meetings and Partings Sixteen short stories *compiled by* Michael Marland
Women *compiled and edited by* Maura Healy
Strange Meeting Susan Hill
Looks and Smiles Barry Hines
A Laurie Lee Selection *edited by* Chris Buckton
P'tang, Yang, Kipperbang and other TV plays Jack Rosenthal
Family Circles Five plays *edited by* Alfred Bradley *and* Alison Leake
Humour and Horror Twelve plays *edited by* Caroline Bennitt
Scene Scripts Four Four television plays *edited by* Alison Leake
A Second Roald Dahl Selection *edited by* Helene Fawcett
Scene Scripts Five Four television plays *edited by* Alison Leake
***Race to be Seen** *edited by* Alison Leake and Mark Wheeler
Festival Plays *edited by* Margaret Mackey
Dash and Defiance *edited by* Alison Leake

Hear me Out *compiled and edited by* Roy Blatchford
A Special Occasion Three plays *edited by* Alison Leake
The Diary of Anne Frank *edited by* Christopher Martin
Wishful Thinking selections from the writings of Keith Waterhou
Intensive Care Four television plays *edited by* Michael Church
The Woman in Black Susan Hill

*Cassette available